WRITING &
RHETORIC

Brett C. McInelly & Brian Jackson

HAYDEN
HM
McNEIL

Hayden-McNeil Sustainability

Hayden-McNeil's standard paper stock uses a minimum of 30% post-consumer waste. We offer higher % options by request, including a 100% recycled stock. Additionally, Hayden-McNeil Custom Digital provides authors with the opportunity to convert print products to a digital format. Hayden-McNeil is part of a larger sustainability initiative through Macmillan Higher Ed. Visit http://sustainability.macmillan.com to learn more.

Printed in the United States of America

10 9 8 7 6 5 4 3 2 1

ISBN 978-0-7380-5878-8

Hayden-McNeil Publishing
14903 Pilot Drive
Plymouth, MI 48170
www.hmpublishing.com

JacksonB 5878-8 F13-S (Writing & Rhetoric Text)

WRITING & RHETORIC

TABLE OF CONTENTS

1

BECOMING A MASTER WRITER

Brian Jackson

MY GOAL FOR THIS CHAPTER IS TO HELP YOU UNDERSTAND THE SIX DOMAINS OF A MASTER WRITER AND TO CONVINCE YOU THAT YOU CAN—AND SURELY WILL—IMPROVE AS A WRITER...IF YOU WANT TO.

Let's talk about LeBron James.

As of this writing, Lebron James, forward for the Miami Heat basketball team, is one of the best basketball players to have ever played the game. He's an NBA champion, a three-time MVP (most valuable player), and a nine-time All Star. He was also Rookie of the Year. He averages around 27 points per game. At the age of 28, he is the youngest player to have scored 20,000 points. Oh, and he's also a two-time Olympic gold medalist.

He has mastered the game at such a level that basketball geeks surely would rank him in the top ten players of all time. In recognition of his mastery, the Miami Heat franchise pays him twenty million dollars a year. I would be Captain Obvious if I said that Lebron James is an *expert* at basketball.

But what makes an *expert* writer? We know why Lebron is considered an expert: He scores more points per game than most players, and he can also pass, rebound, and guard opponents better than many other players. He takes his team to championships. He also has some qualities that are hard to put into words: He has *style*, he has *court presence*, his nickname is "King James," for goodness' sake. What, then, is the "court presence" or "points per game" of a master writer? What are the fundamentals that, like dribbling or rebounding or reading the defense in basketball, set apart the skilled writer from the novice?

And why should these questions even matter to you? You may not think of yourself as a master-writer-in-training, but of course you are. Chances are that no matter what career path you choose, you will end up doing a great deal of writing. I know that's not great news for some of you, but the world we live in runs on communication, and surely it runs better when communication is *good*. For much of your life, regardless of your profession, you'll write emails, proposals, reports, briefs, memos, blog posts, scripts, bids, descriptions, essays, letters, webpages, maybe even books. Add to all this writing the writing you'll do when you're not at work—like SMS texts or social media updates—and you start to understand how important writing is to all of us in our personal, professional, and public lives.

Writing is not just something we do in school: It is a vital means of influence, in all facets of life. The more control you have with it—the more writing skills you can take out of your toolbox—the more influence you'll have over the situations you find yourself in. We connect with each other through writing, improving relationships and forging new ones. Through writing we collaborate, creating new knowledge, new perspectives. Critical conversations take place in writing, and so do essential instructions. Reading the writing of others improves our critical capacities; we learn how to analyze and evaluate. Writing gets everyone on the same page. Writing provokes, writing delights, writing moves and changes minds. Writing helps us learn and think. We learn what we really think when we write, and so do our audiences. Writing is an extension of ourselves, the words and phrases composing avatars of influence. When we master writing, we master our universe.

Maybe that's laying it on a bit thick, but you get the point.

So back to our original question: What makes an *expert* writer? How do we get better at this important thing that apparently we're going to do all the time for the rest of our lives?

Prepare yourself for the shocking news: Research tells us that writers get better by writing. Yes, that's the big secret. To become a master writer, one needs to write, write, write—for various audiences in various situations for various purposes. Writing mastery requires *deliberate practice*, which means many hours of focused, self-aware writing in concrete situations, getting feedback from real people along the way. Though this class will not make you a master writer in the few short weeks of a semester, it will certainly start you on that path by giving you more hours of deliberate practice. By the end of the semester, you'll be closer to becoming a master writer than you are now. It will also give you the tools to *think of yourself* as a writer who is learning, deliberately, how to be better.

The Miami Heat is willing to pay Lebron James the Big Bucks because he has mastered several skill domains necessary for any MVP. He had to learn to dribble, rebound, pass, guard, shoot the long ball, go up against defenders under the basket, dish the ball to teammates when he's double-teamed, and make free throws. Writing, too, requires basic skills (like spelling), but it also requires mastery of at least six major knowledge domains we need to understand to become better writers (see Figure 1). A "knowledge domain" is an area of expertise or know-how, and the ones that follow are based on years of research by writing specialists. I have adapted this list from Anne Beaufort's book *College Writing and Beyond* and John Bean's *Engaging Ideas*.

Let's talk about each learning domain.

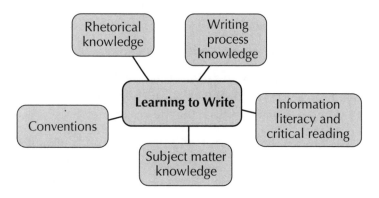

Figure 1. What Makes a Master Writer?

THE DOMAINS OF WRITING EXPERTISE

RHETORICAL KNOWLEDGE

Expert writers understand rhetoric, the study and art of effective communication. The word *rhetoric* comes to us from the Greek word *rhetor* for "speaker." A *rhetor* was someone who spoke to other assembled citizens about problems they all shared. Philosophers began to study how people spoke and to what effect in order to turn speaking into an art and a theory that would give potential speakers real power—to promote shared values, to entertain and delight, to change the course of history with their words. Aristotle, one of the most important philosophers of all time, shares his thinking on this subject in a book titled *On Rhetoric*, in which he gives us a definition: "Let rhetoric be defined as an ability, in each particular case, to see the available means of persuasion" (Kennedy 37). Whether or not you've been aware of it before, you have been practicing rhetoric all your life. Any time you use symbols—like words, hand gestures, even types of clothing—to influence others to feel, think, or do certain things, you are using rhetoric.

You'll learn much more about rhetoric in future chapters, but for now it is important to note that rhetoric is both a *theory* of communication and a *practice*. Rhetoric is a practice because it is something people do. We *use* rhetoric, just like we use language or machines. By theory I mean that rhetoric offers you certain key terms and concepts that are *portable*—that is, they can help you think more carefully about any situation that requires you to write or speak effectively long after you leave this class.

Let me give you an example: Several years ago, a good friend of mine who was studying to be a chaplain in the Army received a letter from the United States military calling him to service in Iraq, where there was still a sizeable U.S. military presence. The timing was unfortunate: He was almost finished with his degree, and deployment would disrupt his process to graduation and create a burden on his wife and two children. So my friend decided to write a letter asking that his tour of duty be deferred until he could finish his degree. What options did he have to make this letter effective?

My friend drew on his understanding of rhetoric. He thought, first, about his **purpose**: What do I want? What am I trying to do? Then he assessed the **situation**: Who is my **audience**, and what do they want? Are they sympathetic to my message, or antagonistic? How can I convince them that their needs and my needs overlap? He then thought about the most **appropriate content** for his letter. (The word *appropriate*, by the way, is a rhetorical term that comes from the Greek work *prepon*, meaning *fitting* or *suitable* to the situation.) My friend wondered what kinds of **appeals** he could use to make his case: Will I use data and strong reasoning, or will I evoke appropriate emotions in my audience, or both? How will I project a responsible, dependable persona? He also thought about his **organization** and **style**: What should I say first, second, third, last, and what kinds of words, phrases, sentence structures, or metaphors should I use? What's the appropriate format for this letter? He wrote the letter, and the military was convinced. He was permitted to defer his deployment until he finished his degree.

Expert writers ask themselves these kinds of questions instinctually when they sit down to write. They ask themselves, "How can I be successful in writing for this particular situation, audience, and moment?" Novice writers struggle at first to make rhetoric an active part of their thinking about communication. For example, we know from research that novice writers write mostly for themselves: they have a difficult time imagining how an audience will read and react to the words on the page/screen. (I bet you've had experiences either writing or receiving writing—in a text message, say, or comment post—that was meant to be friendly but sounds sarcastic or mean.) Sometimes a novice writer's purpose is unclear: novice writers have a hard time answering the question, "What do I want my audience to feel, think, or do?" But as you improve as a writer, rhetorical thinking will become automatic to you. You will know how to use rhetoric to write effectively, and you'll also know how to analyze the rhetoric of other people. Rhetorical knowledge, in short, is the governing domain for all the others.

WRITING PROCESS KNOWLEDGE

Expert writers know how the writing process works—for them and others. In high school, you might have received good grades when you waited to even think about a writing project until the night before it was due. Maybe you tapped out the paper in one sitting, gave it a once-over to search for glaring errors, and turned it in. If that method worked for you, then why fix it?

Because it's a bad method. Really bad. Expert writers know that more writing begets more writing and better writing. The one-time-draft-quickly-and-turn-in method robs you of the chance to grow as a writer because you can't rethink what you've written or get feedback from others. Expert writers know that it takes multiple drafts to complete a persuasive text. They also know, however, that different writing tasks may require different writing strategies; through practice, you sort of fashion your own process. We all brush our teeth differently, but we get the job done. Master writers have developed flexible strategies of thinking about writing, prewriting, drafting, revising, editing, proofreading, and sharing their writing with others for feedback. They know how to use various technologies for writing, so that they can keep track of good ideas and chronicle their progress from draft to draft.

In this class, we will invite you to think more carefully about the process you go through to create writing. In fact, we encourage you to develop *writing strategies* to help you create good writing. Think for a moment about the brain energy required to make a change in our health. As I'm reaching for that second donut I decide, "Brian, it's time to get off your rear end and exercise, maybe drop a few pounds and stave off that first major heart attack." My first move after that painful realization is to commit to a new health regimen by making a *plan.* I decide that I'm going to set aside a specific time three mornings a week to go to the gym. But maybe I'm afraid I'll go once or twice and quit, so I download the phone app called "Gym-Pact" that will actually charge my credit card a fee if I don't go exercise. (Yes, there is such a product.) At any rate, my goal is to reduce my blood pressure and lose ten pounds in the next three months.

These plans I'm making can be called **"self-regulating" strategies**, and you'll need them as a writer. When you get your first writing assignment, you may feel overwhelmed by the task. ("I've never written one of those before… How many pages?… I don't even know where to start!") You'll see a looming deadline and wonder how you will possibly manage to have something ready by then. Self-regulating strategies keep the panic at bay by helping you manage the writing task. Set some goals for yourself, and write them down or tell a roommate about them. ("I will write every day except weekends for at least twenty minutes." "I will shut off my phone and remove all distractions while I write." "I will write in the same place at the same time each day.") Some of these goals may come after you read the assignment carefully or look at the rubric to see what the instructor values. Additionally, talk through *where* and *when* you will write. Set deadlines for yourself, but adjust those deadlines if they don't work for you. Most importantly, reward yourself. ("As soon as I write 500 words, I'll check sports scores on ESPN." "If I write for one hour today, I will go buy myself a mango pineapple smoothie.")

You will also need **writing strategies**. Strategies keep us focused on the task—unless they're "work avoidance" strategies. (Why do I always feel the urgent need to clean my entire house the moment I sit down to write?) In *What Works in Writing Instruction*, BYU English professor Debbie Dean talks about those "invisible" strategies for writing that you may already have, like outlining, brainstorming, drafting on a computer, reading what you've written out loud, using notecards or a digital notecard system, reading, searching databases, blogging, digital bookmarking, looking at examples/models, or talking to people (Dean 4). To make these invisible strategies visible, you should start thinking about what has worked for you in the past and what might be more effective this time. In fact, your instructor may ask you to *reflect* specifically on (1) how you used writing strategies to accomplish your goals, and (2) what you may do differently in the future. This second point is very important. When you are assigned to write something for another class, our hope is that you draw from what you learned in this writing class to start an effective writing process anew.

A final thought about process: Master writers are not afraid to kill what they've already written. Once a rookie gets words on the page, he or she is terrified at the prospect that those words, the product of hours of sweat and tears, might disappear, to be replaced by even more words. Since master writers write every day—yes, *every day*—they are not as scared of taking what they've written and throwing it in the recycling bin. More—and better—words will come. Trust your inner writer to emerge!

INFORMATION LITERACY AND CRITICAL READING

Expert writers know how to ask questions, find information, assess that information, and repurpose it for new rhetorical situations. Master writers support their own words with the words and authority of other writers. They take their questions to the Web, to the library, to databases, and other people. They know how to narrow a topic based on their goals, and they know how to sift through lots of possible resources swiftly and effectively.

Once they find useful sources, expert writers are expert *readers*. They keep their purpose in mind and employ flexible reading strategies so that they waste little time passing their eyes over every single word of a text. They know what to read *for*. In other words, they know how to find the main point, the support, the methods, the conclusions and implications so they can blend their writing with the writing of others. They also know how to evaluate a text for authority, timeliness, relevance, and bias, among other things. In other words, they read *rhetorically*. They analyze how texts function in various rhetorical situations, and they can evaluate the way a writer uses appeals and various strategies of language.

Subject Matter Knowledge

Expert writers know quite a bit about the subject they're writing about. In fact, research shows that the more someone knows about a topic, the easier the cognitive task of writing becomes. Unfortunately, in first-year writing subject mastery is a challenge. Many of you are straight out of high school without much coursework in a specific discipline. And that's fine. You are likely familiar at least with the research paper. Often research papers are little more than data dumps: Look, teacher, at all the stuff I know about the state of Alaska! While expert writers may know quite a bit about the subject, they also know how to enter a conversation about topics they write about: they know what has been said about the topic and what kinds of questions or problems must be addressed. In fact expert writers know that sometimes the subject matter is less important than the questions or problems the writer asks that can be answered with research into a subject.

Your writing class may focus on a specific topic for analysis or research, but even then, several weeks is not much time to master a topic. Hopefully this challenge will prompt you to learn all you can about the topics you write about or, if you have the option, write about what you know.

CONVENTIONS

Expert writers have mastered the conventions appropriate to the rhetorical situation. A *convention* is an agreed-upon principle, an expectation shared by a particular community. It's how we agree how to do things. There are all kinds of conventions that govern cultural practices (think dating), and it isn't always clear who sets the conventions or if we all just decide, through trial and error, that that's the way it is. But expert writers will understand which conventions are important for a given situation; they'll also know when conventions should be broken for rhetorical effect.

Here are the conventions that you should know about as a writer:

> *Genre*: a genre is a semi-standardized way of responding to a recurring situation or need. A genre is a type of text or other cultural artifact that takes a recognizable form. Think about movies. Do you like horror movies, or comedies? Or thrillers, tragedies, or romances? These categories are genres; they take predictable forms based on the situations that bring them forth. Writing, too, most often appears in a particular genre. It has a certain shape, organization, design, style, argument. If you go into the sciences, you will need money to fund your research projects, and you get money by writing a grant proposal, which is a genre. Scientists also write research articles for peer-reviewed journals, lab reports, emails, and other various genres that they have learned to write by belonging to a specific community of knowledge-makers.
>
> Master writers are genre thinkers. Before they ask *what will I write?*, they ask *in what genre will I write?* The answer to the genre question depends on the needs of the readers who belong to a shared community to which the writer also belongs. (We often call these communities *discourse communities.*) Sometimes in college you will have to write papers that don't have a very clear genre. Like a "research paper." What's that? Who writes "research papers"? The answer is, writing students. Some writing scholars believe it is useful to think of the papers you write in college as *antecedent*

genres, or genres that will prepare you to write in more specific genres later. The point is that when you get a writing assignment, think about the genre you are being asked to write in.

Grammar. How would you define grammar? There are at least three possibilities.

1. Grammar is the system of putting words together, a system you have mastered naturally since childhood. It is a remarkable fact of nature that in most cases, you do not need to teach children how to speak in grammatically sound sentences; they just learn it by listening to the people they live with. Grammar, then, is the system inside our heads that tells us to put "big" before "red" and "red" before "tractor" when we say "big red tractor." (That was one of my son's favorites phrases when he was a toddler.)

2. But grammar is also the system of rules we learn, particularly when we learn how to write in school or how to speak another language. If you were to write, "Each of the teachers have a college degree," someone might step in with a red pen and cross out the word *have* and write *has,* because the word *each* is a singular pronoun. The red pen may also swoop down if you write the following as a complete sentence: "Each of the teachers with a college degree." We call that a *sentence fragment.* The point is that grammar is also a set of rules governing language. Sometimes the rules make obvious sense (the word "red" goes before the word "tractor"), but sometimes they don't (do not end a sentence with a preposition). Sometimes they change. Sometimes we obey grammatical principles more out of etiquette than fear of the nonexistent Grammar Police. An expert writer understands the rules so that she can sound intelligent in writing. When we commit multiple errors, readers have to work harder to understand us; they may form inaccurate impressions of us. As arbitrary as the rules can be, our readers still expect us to abide by them—or wow them when we don't.

3. Finally, grammar is *rhetorical power*. You can use prin-
    ciples of grammar to add variety, tone, balance, and
    oomph to your writing. You can create emotion and
    expectation in your readers with grammatical flair.

Punctuation: All those dots, dashes, smudges, and squiggles
that garnish your writing—that's punctuation. Thousands
of years ago, punctuation was a method for helping actors
learn how to deliver their lines. Now punctuation has hard-
ened into a system of practices that helps us create variety
and contrast in writing. But punctuation, like grammar,
changes over time. The hyphen, for example, seems to be
going out of style, and the "oxford comma"—the comma
that goes after that second-to-last item in a series—has been
dropped from usage. Master writers pay attention to such
changes, or they find peer reviewers that will help them pay
attention.

Document design: Each document invites you to *compose* it,
using text and image to create a feel for the document. But
documents also have conventions for style. Where do you
put your title or name? Where does the text go, and what
font type will you use or *can* you use? Can you put images
in your document? Where? Will you use page numbers,
bold or italicized text, headings, single or double spac-
ing, text wrap? What multimodal affordances come with
each genre? How creative can you be? These questions, of
course, depend on the rhetorical situation, but the master
writer knows how to use effective design principles even for
standard double-spaced academic papers.

Documentation methods: There are conventions for citing
sources, too. These conventions are often canonized in big
books like *The Chicago Manual of Style* or the *Modern Language Association Handbook*. When you settle on a major, you
will start writing in the discipline that major represents,
and that discipline will have a handbook with instructions
about how to cite and list sources. Master writers have an
obvious command over documentation methods.

Your instructor may talk more about conventions I haven't mentioned here (like usage, sexist language, or mechanics). For all the conventions I've listed, the most important point is to know, simply, that there are conventions embedded in rhetorical situations, and your power as a writer will depend in part on how well you know and use them.

Learning How to Write

Learning how to write is the sixth and final domain of the master writer. The speed and depth of your learning depends on how well you can learn to step back and think about your thinking. Some learning specialists call this "self-efficacy," and as corny as it sounds, it is a vital part of learning to write. Your instructor will encourage you to reflect on how you're doing as an apprentice writer and what you need to do to improve.

You might find the above list intimidating. (I have to master *how many* domains?) I understand the concern. But relax: You're just setting out. Learning to be a master writer is a life-long process that will challenge you in every new rhetorical situation. The kinds of writing you do in first-year writing may not be the kind of writing you learn to do in your discipline. And when you start a career, you'll need to learn how to write all over again for various audiences in various genres for various situations. And you will master writing in each new situation if you remember the principles we talked about in this chapter. (See the appendix to this chapter for more questions that will help you for each new writing situation.)

A final word on learning to write. Writing—and I ain't tellin' you anything new here—is *hard.* It's a challenging cognitive task. Not only do you need mastery of basic mechanical skills like typing or spelling, you also need to hold in your mind simultaneously your purpose, your audience, and the text you are writing. Experts tell us that you need to clock around 10,000 hours of deliberate practice in something before you master it. LeBron didn't just pick up a basketball when he was bored; he had to work at it. Even after being recognized as the NBA's MVP, he actually flew down to Houston to meet with

Hakeem Olajuwan, a retired NBA hall-of-famer, to learn how to play more aggressive offense. Mastery takes years. In other words, don't plan on mastering powerfully persuasive writing in the few years you'll be in college, let alone the few weeks you have in a writing class.

That said, I want to be your cheerleader here as you start your writing class. Though improving your writing will be hard work, it will be rewarding. And the good news is that *anyone can improve their writing.* Anyone, with focused practice and hard work, can improve as a writer. Good writing skills are not innate, like height. When some people tell me "I'm just not good at writing," it's as if they're saying, "I'm just not six feet tall, and I'll never be six feet tall." That may be true for height, but it's not true for writing. You can, and will, improve as a writer if you set some clear writing goals, seek feedback from your instructor and peers, and commit to the hard, rewarding work of writing—every day.

I've heard it said before that writing is never really perfect, only due. As writers, we work toward perfection without ever actually reaching it. In some ways, writing mastery is like an *asymptote* in algebra. That's the line that a curve approaches but never touches. Daniel Pink, author of the book *Drive,* explains that mastery is "a source of allure... The joy is in the pursuit more than the realization" (Pink 125).

We hope you will feel some of that joy as you improve your rhetorical powers through writing.

APPENDIX TO CHAPTER ONE

Deliberate writing practice requires more than just muddling through writing tasks. Although each writing task is different, the following list of questions will help you in your deliberate practice as writer. To avoid assaulting you with hundreds of questions, I've decided to focus on rhetorical knowledge and writing process knowledge, since those two domains tend to govern the others. These questions will help you think through any writing task you face during college and beyond. Commit them to memory, if you can, so the questions will serve as heuristics (tools of discovery) in the future.

Your instructor may have you respond to these questions in writing before, during, or after a major writing assignment.

Rhetorical Knowledge

- What is my purpose for writing? What do I want to accomplish?

- Who is my audience? How much do I know about them? What are their needs, values, culture, experience, and interests? How do our needs and interests overlap or diverge?

- Why is this issue timely? What has happened in the past to make this topic interesting, current, controversial? What are the multiple perspectives at play?

- What genre do I need to write in? How much do I know about this genre? How do I need to organize my writing? What kind of tone or style is possible in this genre?

- What kinds of claims, reasons, assumptions, and evidence will be appropriate and convincing? What emotional appeals will be most useful in this situation?

- What kind of *person* is most convincing to this audience? How can I become that person in my writing? What *concessions* or *counter-arguments* do I need to address to convince my audience?

Writing Process Knowledge

Self-Assessment

- What is this assignment asking me to do? Have I written a paper like this before? How good am I at writing these kinds of papers?

- Have I read the assignment sheet? What remaining questions do I have?

- What are my strengths as a writer? Weaknesses?

- What are my usual writing methods? How have they worked in the past? What do I need to change about my writing process to make it more effective?

- How do I think I'll do on this paper? What do I hope this paper will help me do in the future?

- What kind of writer do I want to become?

Writing Strategies

- What writing strategies will I use to produce writing? Will I outline, freewrite, chunk, brainstorm, talk about my topic with other people?

- What has worked for me in the past?

- Which writing strategies that I learn in class will I try on my own?

- What do I need to read to understand this assignment better? What outside texts? What kind of research do I need to do to prepare to write? And how will I take notes on my reading?

- [After peer review and/or teacher comments]: What is the feedback asking me to do? What part of the feedback is most useful to me? What is least useful? Moving forward, what do I need to change? What needs to stay the same?

Self-Regulating Strategies

- Where will I write? When will I write? How much each day?

- When is the first, second, third thing due? What is my first deadline?

- What are my goals for this assignment?

- How will I keep myself from getting distracted? How will I reward myself for writing?

- Who will look at my writing?

- When will I give a draft to my instructor?

Reflection

- What strategies did I use on this writing assignment that worked well for me? (Debbie Dean) Why did they work?

- When do I think I'd use these strategies again?

- What was the hardest or most challenging part about this writing assignment?

- What did I learn from writing this paper? What did I learn about myself as a writer? What's left to learn/improve on?

- What do I think I did well in this paper? What not so well? What do my previous two answers tell me about next time?

REFERENCES

Bean, John. *Engaging Ideas.* 2nd ed. San Francisco: Jossey-Bass, 2011.

Beaufort, Anne. *College Writing and Beyond.* Logan: Utah State UP, 2007.

Dean, Deborah. *What Works in Writing Instruction.* Urbana, IL: NCTE, 2010.

Pink, Daniel. *Drive.* NY: Riverhead, 2009.

NOTES

NOTES

NOTES

Chapter 2

WRITING
AN ARGUMENT

Brian Jackson

My goal for this chapter is to help you understand what an argument is and how to make one.

One time while on a hike with friends in the Wasatch Mountains, near Salt Lake City, Utah, I found myself stuck in a stupid argument. I'm sure you've had a few of those yourself, so you might empathize. As usual, we were arguing about something we knew nothing about: the United States Army Reserves. Who knows how we got on the subject. My friend was arguing that it was far better to have your best troops in the Reserves instead of on the front lines of battle. I was arguing—who knows why—that if your best troops were in the Reserves, you risked getting trounced abroad where your weaker soldiers struggled, and it was far better to fight and win wars overseas with your best than be forced to defend your own soil with your best. Naturally!

It got pretty heated, our little debate on the mountain trail. I should have known it would: I'd had heated debates with this friend since we met in fourth grade, including one in which we almost started punching each other over whether the science fiction technology from the movie *Back to the Future II* actually existed. But even though we failed to convince each other that our take on the Army Reserves was the right one, and even though our reasoning was naive and uninformed, we were still getting something done by having a debate. As our argument proceeded through the back and forthness of everyday talk among friends, it *clarified* positions, *revealed* weaknesses in reasoning, and *sharpened* our analytical abilities. The argument, though sloppy, taught us something about something.

The word **argument** often has negative connotations. Say the word out loud—what's your first impression? An uncomfortable disagreement? Fighting? Political adversaries on the streets with forehead veins pulsing? A domestic disturbance? If you write "argument" in Google Image, most of the pictures you'll see are of people getting in each others' faces, shouting at each other with their teeth clenched, spit flying, eyeballs almost popping out.

These are unfortunate connotations.

An argument is so much more, and better, than a fight. In this course we will use the word *argument* to describe a rhetorical strategy that everyone uses to get stuff done in the world. The word comes from the Old French *arguer* from Latin *argutari*, meaning "to make clear, prove, assert." An argument, then, is an assertion—a **claim**—that is accompanied by an attempt to prove or support the claim. Let's call this support a **reason**. When a parent asks a teenager why he is coming home late and he says, "I lost track of time," he is providing an argument: I am late (the *claim*) because I lost track of time (the *reason*). From the parent's perspective, it's a lame argument, but it has the essential elements of our definition of argument: **a claim supported by a reason to accept the claim.**

We need to understand that second part—the *reason*—to understand argument as a rhetorical strategy. I once overheard a female student talking on the phone about a romantic movie she had seen the night before called *The Vow*. It was clear by her tortured voice that she had been disappointed in the movie. She even said as much: "I was so looking forward to it, and it was just really disappointing!" Had she made an argument?

Nope. At least not at that point. All I heard was a claim: *The Vow* is disappointing. Of course the obvious question to any claim is *why*? But this student didn't let me down. After expressing her disappointment with sighs and groans she said, "The ending was so bad! It totally didn't resolve anything and just kinda left you hanging." The *reason* completes the argument. It invites us—the audience—to accept or reject the claim and agree with the arguer.

There is power in an argument. In fact, there is scientific evidence that arguing is a healthy trait we humans have adapted to help us deal with the truckload of information dumped on us each day. We use arguments naturally to justify who we are and what we do. We come up with claims and reasons to support our decisions and encourage others to see things our way. We analyze arguments that challenge our beliefs, values, or well being. Recently in the journal *Behavioral and Brain Sciences*, Hugo Mercier and Dan Sperber argued that argument is central to the way we think. In fact, they *argue*—fittingly!—that the primary function of thinking itself is to produce and analyze arguments.

One last note on the idea of argument before we move on. It has no doubt occurred to you that argument is central to rhetoric—the art of persuasion and social cooperation. It is also central, as rhetoric itself is, to democratic life. Democracy depends on the judgment of the citizens—it's a scary thought, I know, but we're all we've got. And we cannot exercise good judgment to make good decisions about life if we do not hear arguments—not only good ones, but bad ones as well—about what we should be doing and why we should be doing it. All the crucial political questions that almost flummox us and grind the gears of government to a halt—*What should we do about the nation's uninsured? What if an enemy of state produces a nuclear weapon? How should the wealthy be taxed? How do we improve the schools? How do we get more people into college? How much should the Internet be regulated? What do we want from our media?*—need answers, and those answers take the form of arguments: claims, supported by reasons.

INVENTING ARGUMENTS THE OLD SCHOOL WAY

In the course of your life, you will be asked to make arguments about this and that. Sometimes you'll have to make an argument in the spur of the moment without much preparation. One time while my wife and I were on a walk, she told me she wanted to replace the windows in the house, and she asked me what I thought about it. She might as well have asked me what I thought about carbon nanotubes or gluten-free diets or Sumerian architecture or anything else I had spent exactly zero minutes thinking about. Any argument I could make would be on the fly, without any analytical thought or research. We all have to make such arguments from time to time.

In writing classes, however, you have the luxury of crafting your arguments in advance by going through a rigorous writing process involving *rhetorical invention*. Yes, crafting arguments is a creative act—an act of invention! You're going to pull the raw materials of persuasion out of thin air and *presto!*—create a compelling argument that no mere mortal will be able to withstand. Or at least that's what you hope.

So how does one *invent* arguments? One method, or series of methods, comes to us from classical rhetoric. As was mentioned in the introductory chapter, rhetoric has always been a human practice—like dance and worship and battle. But the ancient Greeks made rhetoric an art that could be studied, taught, and perfected. In *On Rhetoric*, Aristotle argued that rhetoric is the process by which we find the "available means of persuasion." We do that through strategies of invention.

If you already know what your argument will be about, you begin inventing an argument by imagining an audience. (You'll get more on audience in chapter four.) What do you know about your audience? How much can you discover about their interests and needs? What are your overlapping interests? How much do you already agree on? Your instructor will help you think carefully about your audience in relation to the rhetorical task he or she has assigned you. But one general rule is this: imagine that your audience is initially hostile to or skeptical of your argument and that they need to be convinced. This little imagination exercise will help you refine your argument to make it the best you can.

(The next step would be to choose an appropriate genre for your argument, but I'll assume that your instructor will assign the genre.)

Once you have a sense of your audience and an idea for a possible topic/claim, one way to invent claims is to think about them as answers to questions—very big questions, in fact. Questions like:

What exists? And what kind of *stuff* is it made of?

What is good?

What should we do?

Wow—deep. But hey, almost every claim you hear is going to fall into one of these three categories, so they can be useful to know. Let's give them specific names and flesh them out a bit.

What exists? And what kind of *stuff* is it made of? Let's call this kind of claim a *substance* claim. (You'll notice some overlap between these principles and the one Kristine Hansen will teach you in Chapter 7.) Substance claims make claims about the nature of reality, about facts, about the status of things, about history and events, about definitions and essences. If I make the claim that humans cause climate change by burning fossil fuels, I'm making a substance claim. If I argue that political campaign contributions are "free speech," that's a substance claim, too. If I claim that bicycle riders on campus pose a danger to other students, or that baseball is a religion, or that no cinnamon gum lasts longer than Big Red, or that it is impossible to balance the national budget without raising taxes, or that the public schools are in crisis, then I'm making a substance claim.

What is good? This kind of claim is a *quality* or *value* claim. Quality claims are statements about what is good or bad, right or wrong, ought or ought not, moral or immoral, effective or ineffective, best or worst, righteous or wicked, dumb or smart, cool or lame, ethical or otherwise. It's wrong to eat animals for any reason, says a quality claim. And a quality claim answers right back: Eating beef is a good old-fashioned American tradition! A quality claim calls a movie—like *The Vow*—disappointing or an action—like downloading copyrighted music outside legal channels—immoral. This candidate is better than that one. Vampires are not as cool as werewolves. It's justifiable to start a war if there's a credible threat. The cost of parking on campus is a scandal. Sexist remarks are cowardly. Tax cuts for the wealthy are good for the economy. You get the point.

What should we do? My wife argues that we should replace the windows in the house. I argue that we shouldn't. At least we agree on what we disagree about, and what we disagree about is what we should do, which we call a *policy* or *procedure* claim. Policy claims are statements about things that should be done. Think of the way our legislature (ideally!) approaches a problem. What should we do about rising health care costs? Require everyone to have insurance, answers one group; another claims that we should reduce frivolous malpractice lawsuits. Should the university prohibit skateboards on campus? Should your instructor give everyone A's this semester?

In argument practice, some of these kinds of claims bleed together. Someone, for example, might use what we call a substance claim as *the reason* to support a policy claim. An example: We should remove the emergency phones on campus because every student now has a cell phone. Since arguments are made up of two assertions—we've been calling them claim and reason—the two parts can be categorized differently, and most likely are. It probably wouldn't be very effective to support a policy claim with a policy reason: *We should replace the windows because we should conserve energy.* As I mentioned above, a more effective argument will support a claim with good data: *We should replace the windows because the cheap ones we now have lose 45% of the heat in the house.* The point is that it's helpful to think of your argument in terms of these three categories.

What other methods can you use to invent arguments? The ancient rhetoricians of Greece and Rome had a little trick called *topoi* to help them invent as many arguments as possible in the "drafting" stage of an argument. *Topoi* is the plural form of the Greek word *topos*, or place. *Topoi* are places you go in your mind when you want to invent an argument but you're not sure how.

Put simply, *topoi* are categories of thought. Each category helps us see an issue from a different perspective, thus helping us generate lots of good material for an argument we're trying to write. Some people translate *topoi* into the English word *topics*, but that might confuse us because we think of the word topic as a subject or issue, as in, "What was the topic of their conversation?"

In *Teaching the Argument in Writing*, argument scholar Richard Fulkerson uses the acronym GASCAP to teach *topoi*, and that's a great place for us to start (again, more later). Now, let's pretend we want to write an argument on health issues for students. Let's say we want to look into the nutrition and dietary behavior of freshmen on college campuses. Here's an example of how the GASCAP principles can help you generate ideas for arguments. As you read these examples, think about what makes this kind of argument strong and what might make it seem weak.

G is for *generalization*. If a sample group has X trait, then the bigger group has X trait. This kind of argument depends on whether the sample is really representative of the population. (If you go on a date with a loud, obnoxious male student, are you justified in thinking all male students are the same? Would that conclusion be justified after two, three, ten similar dates with different men?)

> *Example:* If students at Brigham Young University eat more empty calories during finals week than they do at any time in the semester, then we can assume college students nationally do the same.

A is for *analogy*. X and Y are alike enough that if X has Z traits, then Y likely has Z traits. Again, this argument's strength rests on similarity—this time between two alike things or groups. For you poets out there, metaphor functions like this. If I compare thee to a summer's day, I'm arguing that summer's days have certain qualities that you, too, possess.

> *Example:* If students at the University of Texas eat more empty calories during finals week, then we can assume that BYU students do the same.

S is for *sign.* X means that Y is the case. If there's smoke, there's fire. If she doesn't call you back, she's just not interested. If a straight-A student starts blowing off class and assignments mid-semester, I may suspect that something has gone wrong in his or her personal life—but then again, I may be reading the signs incorrectly.

> *Example.* BYU freshmen tend to gain around seven pounds during their freshman year. (This may or may not be the case, by the way; I made it up.) The weight gain is a sign that the students' diets change significantly once they move out of their parents' home.

C is for *causality.* X caused Y, or Y is a consequence of X. A tricky one sometimes. After a horrible school shooting in Columbine, Colorado in 1999, journalists tried to argue that hard rock music, video games, bullying, or parenting caused two young men to bring guns to school and murder their classmates. Was that really the case? Causal or consequential arguments appeal to us because they suggest sequences that seem to make sense. Our brains demand connections. Some of them are sound, some are not.

> *Example.* Students who play more video games than other students tend to drink more soda than other students.

A is for *authority.* If an expert on a given issue says X, then X is probably true. Well, who's an expert? Someone who knows quite a bit about a subject or who has spent a significant amount of time working in a particular field, OR someone who has intimate experience with the subject, OR someone who has some kind of credential related to the subject (like a PhD in microbiology), OR someone who is just nationally recognized as an authority on a subject. Authorities are strong insofar as the audience accepts them as legitimate.

> *Example.* The *New England Journal of Medicine* reports that college students who play two or more hours of video games a day consume three times more soda than the national average (Yeah, I made that up, too. But doesn't it sound authoritative?).

P is for *principle*. X is true or just or right or moral. Notice that you now have three terms for this kind of claim: quality, value, or principle. These kinds of arguments depend on what values are shared between the writer and the audience. Think about the various ways of thinking that create moral judgments: religion, politics, philosophy, culture, intuition. Things can get tricky in there. Psychology professor Jonathan Haidt has argued that moral judgments, though powerful, are sometimes difficult to defend because they come from deep within the strange mazes of our intuition. And yet, so many of our public arguments come from the moral or ethical realm.

> *Example:* It makes sense for the administration to provide more healthy options in the cafeteria because we should be concerned with the health of the students.

Kristine Hansen will give you more tools for invention in chapter seven. For now, the point is to learn to *systematically* blitz your issue with as many questions and principles you possibly can to find an effective argument that will persuade your audience. But how do you know what makes an effective argument for your audience?

This is quite a vexing question. What do I mean by the word "effective"? One answer might be, "Whatever persuades your audience!" *Effective*, in other words, is *audience-specific*, based on what rhetorical theorist Gerard Hauser calls "local norms of reasonableness." An argument that might convince a convention of evangelicals in Texas might not convince readers of a physics blog. Each **discourse community** has a different way of creating knowledge and making arguments, and sometimes those ways are very specific, even exclusionary.

However, this answer, though probably true to the way rhetoric works at times, is in some ways unsatisfactory. For one thing, it seems to suggest that the point of rhetoric is to use whatever arguments will convince a specific audience, and no one else. If it works to scare people, make wild and unsupportable claims, stereotype, lie, attack others, or misrepresent an opposing view, well…then it works! While it is true that very specific discourse communities will have their own way of arguing, in public discourse we are *ethically obligated* to pursue the public good through our arguments—in other words, to make arguments, with good reasons, that help to refine, rather than dull, public judgment. Your challenge is to grow in rhetorical knowledge by devising reasonable, emotionally salient arguments that even people who disagree with you might accept.

In that spirit, then, we can say that there are ways we have come to evaluate arguments that depend on general principles of reasoning—principles that, though general, work in specific situations as well. We can think of arguments as *strong* or *weak*, depending on whether they have certain virtues of good thinking. In the next chapter, we'll review some principles that will help you understand how to determine whether an argument is strong or weak.

EXERCISES

1. Provide reasons for the following claims (and identify whether the claim is a substance, quality, or policy claim):

   - You should get a haircut.

   - Kissing in public is wrong.

   - Facebook friendships are more superficial than face-to-face friendships.

   - The University should require all incoming freshmen to buy a tablet (like an iPad).

2. Use the three claim categories and GASCAP to come up with arguments for the following topics:

   - general education requirements

   - college athletics

   - tuition/pell grants/student loans

   - college student housing rules

   - "helicopter parents" (parents who are too involved in the lives of their college kids)

3. What do you think makes an argument strong or weak, effective or ineffective? Talk about this question with your class or a classmate.

REFERENCES

Fulkerson, Richard. *Teaching the Argument in Writing.* Urbana, IL: NCTE, 1996.

Hauser, Gerard. *Introduction to Rhetorical Theory.* 2nd ed. Prospect Heights, IL: Waveland P, 2002.

NOTES

NOTES

NOTES

Chapter 3

ANALYZING AN ARGUMENT

Brian Jackson

MY GOAL FOR THIS CHAPTER IS TO HELP YOU THINK AND READ CRITICALLY BY LEARNING HOW TO IDENTIFY AND EVALUATE THE PARTS OF AN ARGUMENT.

Arguments are sometimes obvious, sometimes not. The female student—the one I mentioned in the previous chapter that I overheard on the phone—makes an explicit argument: The movie *The Vow* is a bad movie because it has an unresolved ending. Whether this is a strong argument or a weak one, at least it's obviously an argument, according to our C + R definition. We have a claim and a reason for supporting that claim. But sometimes people make *implicit* arguments that you, the rhetorical critic, have to reconstruct in your mind. For example, in the restroom at the Monterrey Bay Aquarium I saw this sign on the paper towel dispenser:

PAPER TOWELS = TREES

What do you make of that? Paper towels are trees? What was the aquarium trying to tell me?

No doubt you have already reconstructed the argument in your head. Maybe it goes something like this:

Claim: When drying your hands, you should use as few paper towels as possible…

Reason: …because these paper towels are made from a natural resource.

This argument is hidden implicitly in the PAPER TOWELS = TREES sign. It's up to the audience to reconstruct the argument and accept or reject it. But why should anyone accept this argument?

Alas, this is a complicated question. If arguments were like mathematical equations, then the problem of persuasion would be solved: As long as the audience accepts the definition of the numbers and other math symbols, then the conclusion is inevitable. The same goes for logical *syllogisms.* A syllogism is a logical statement of two claims, called premises, and a conclusion. If the premises are true, then the conclusion is obvious. Here's an example:

Premise #1: All humans will die.

Premise #2: You are a human.

Conclusion: Therefore, you will die.

Bad news, I know. But if premises #1 and #2 are true—and I'm pretty sure they are—then the conclusion follows. In fact, it follows with a kind of *violence* because there's no way for you to reject it and remain a rational person. Face it: You're gonna die.

But everyday arguments don't really take the form of a syllogism, nor are they *logical* in the philosophical sense of that word. Rather, they are *rhetorical.* Take our movie critic. Her first premise is *The Vow is a bad movie.* Well, maybe! Unlike in the *All humans will die* example, we need to be persuaded with good reasons before we will accept that *The Vow* is a bad movie and get on the same page as the arguer or speaker. Master writers understand how this process works; they can analyze arguments by dissecting claims, reasons, and assumptions.

Let's go back to the PAPER TOWELS = TREES argument for a moment. How could we analyze the argument as we reconstructed it above? We can't really confront the claim because the claim by itself isn't an argument. So let's look at the other parts of the argument.

1. The first thing we could do is **question the reason**. Notice that the reason (*paper towels are made from a natural resource*) to accept the claim (*When drying your hands...*) is a fact-based claim in itself—a substance claim (see Chapter 2). The arguer is telling me, as my drippy hands reach for the dispenser, that to make paper towels for restrooms, someone has to go out and chop down a tree. Is that really true? Who knows! Maybe paper towels are made from recycled materials or cloth or wood pulp, or maybe very few trees are used in the process, or maybe trees are used to make paper towels but not "these towels"—the ones in the Monterrey Bay Aquarium. The point is that you can begin analyzing an argument by checking to see whether the reason is a fact we can depend on. In this case, since I have nothing but the Monterrey Bay Aquarium authorities to rely on, I'm going to go ahead and assume they're right about where paper towels come from. (Do you agree?)

    Granted, assessing the facts is far easier when you have a statement like "these paper towels are made from a natural resource" than when you have, as in our movie critic example, a statement like "the ending doesn't resolve things." Seems like a subjective statement to me. If *I* were to throw caution and good taste to the wind and go see *The Vow*, would *I* think that the ending didn't resolve things? When it comes to these kinds of judgments, sometimes we must depend on the *ethos* or authority of the speaker to help us determine whether or not to accept this reason. (More on ethos in a later chapter.) But in sum, your first task as a rhetorical critic is to analyze the reason and determine whether the reason is a fact—something you could look up and confirm—or some other kind of assertion.

2. The second, and more challenging, way to assess an argument is to **look at the *assumptions* that make the argument possible**. But assumptions are hard to "look" at, because usually they're not there. Assumptions are the (often) unspoken values, beliefs, or principles that arguers assume they share with their audience. In the case of the movie critic, the unspoken underlying assumption could look like this:

Assumption: Movies that have endings that don't resolve things are bad.

You may have thought of other ways to express this assumption that go deeper into underlying assumptions. You could say that as movie audiences we expect a certain structure to our movie plots, and the structure gives us a kind of pleasure, which drives us back to the theaters. When a movie violates that structure contract—say, by concluding in a manner that leaves too many loose ends—it should be condemned. We've gone way beyond where I think the student movie critic was going, but these assumptions seem to underlie her argument. She means to express them without saying them because she assumes that her audience assumes them, too. And it's our job as the audience to analyze whether her assumptions are legitimate.

Analyzing assumptions is challenging, but sometimes it's the only way we can assess whether or not an argument is strong or weak. Let's go back to the paper towels argument:

Claim: When drying your hands, you should use as few paper towels as possible...

Reason: ...because these paper towels are made from a natural resource.

What does the speaker/writer/Aquarium staff assume is true in this case? One way to express the unspoken assumption might be:

Assumption: Natural resources should be conserved or used sparingly.

With the assumption now on the table, can we say whether this is a good/bad, strong/weak argument?

Sigh: It depends. It depends, of course, on the audience and whether the audience accepts the reasons, data, and assumptions. But in this case I'll take a chance and say that this assumption probably enjoys quite a bit of *adherence* in public discourse. Adherence in argument studies means *agreement.* Many people, I'd guess, agree that natural resources should be conserved or used sparingly. So maybe I want to conclude that since the assumption is strong— i.e., enjoys widespread adherence—then this argument is strong.

But not so fast. A rhetorical critic doesn't let assumptions off the hook that easy. We may go further and ask this assumption a "why" question: *Why should natural resources be conserved?* What if trees are so plentiful that they don't need to be conserved? Now we're getting into a third strategy for analyzing arguments:

3. Finally, you can rebut the claim by **coming up with a counter-claim**. We've looked at the reason and the assumption, and now we should test the argument by coming up with possible rebuttals. We've already done some of that work above by asking whether the paper towels in the dispenser actually come from trees. Think about rebuttals as "unless" statements that cast doubt on the argument.

When drying your hands, you should use as few paper towels as possible because these paper towels are made from a natural resource...

...*unless* they *aren't* made from a natural resource.

...*unless* we don't need to conserve trees because there are so many of them.

....*unless* conserving trees will be too expensive or have other negative consequences—on the economy, for example.

As a budding rhetorician, you should practice identifying claims, reasons, assumptions, and rebuttals in the arguments you hear each day. Like right now. Take a moment and analyze a recent argument you heard, read, or participated in.

ANALYZING ARGUMENTS IN WRITING

How to analyze based on audience. Remember that as a rhetorical critic, you are not analyzing the *logic* of an argument independent of the argument's rhetorical situation. Arguments are directed at audiences in specific situations for specific reasons. When you analyze an argument, you are acting as a representative of a *rhetorical audience*—the audience for which the argument is intended. And actually, you have two options for this: You can analyze an argument based on [1] the actual audience intended by the writer—let's call it the **primary audience**, or [2] the implied audience of educated, interested people, including yourself, even if you weren't the audience directly intended by the argument—which we'll call the **secondary audience**. But a caution: If you are writing an argument analysis, you want to convince *your own* audience that you are not analyzing an argument simply as an act of personal opinion. You can't just say an argument is weak because you think it's stupid.

Let's look at an example that illustrates this dual audience phenomenon. In 1997 David Fleming wrote an article for *Sports Illustrated* titled "Wrestling's Dirty Secret." In the article, Fleming argued that the National Collegiate Athletic Association should crack down on weight loss practices that endanger college wrestlers who have to fit into a certain weight category to compete. (What kind of claim is this, folks?) He argues that the "drastic weight loss" athletes go through is akin to torture; the NCAA is responsible for putting a stop to it. So before we can analyze this claim—with its reasons and assumptions—we'll have to place the argument in its **rhetorical situation**, a term you'll learn more about in the next chapter. For now, we ask: Who is the audience for David Fleming's argument?

Let's say there are *two* possible audiences. First, there is the primary audience—the immediate audience for which the argument is intended. Who is the primary audience for "Wrestling's Dirty Secret?" The readers of *Sports Illustrated* in 1997. Who are they? Well, unless you want to do some kind of database research, you're going to have to make some assumptions based on your own experience with media demographics. We can assume, for example, that many—most?—*SI* readers are male. How much further can we go than that? Can we guess an age set? Do young men read *SI* more than old men? How about race or socioeconomic background? Or political leanings? I don't think I'm willing to launch guesses on these points, so we might be stuck with mostly male, maybe (vaguely!) younger than older. We may also want to look into what was happening around December 1997 that would have made this argument *kairotic* or timely. (More on *kairos* in another chapter.) If you wanted to research this further, you could look at back issues of *SI* and make some audience inferences based on the advertisements. Maybe Google would cough up more specific readership details.

So much for the primary audience. There's also a secondary audience that includes anyone who actually reads the argument, at any point in time. The secondary audience also includes anyone who might be interested in the topic and/or anyone who the writer thinks might be persuaded by the message. Thinking about audience this way is rewarding: It makes YOU, the reader, part of the action. Fleming's argument is addressed to you and to anyone, any time, who might be interested in an argument about the NCAA and its policies about student athletes. In the article itself, Fleming begins with a moving account of the death of one college wrestler who tried to lose seventeen pounds in three days. This kind of emotional appeal is directed to anyone concerned about the well being of student athletes. (Is that you?)

How does this dual perspective of audience change the way you analyze an argument? Significantly. First, it brings you into the rhetorical situation, making you a judge of the persuasiveness of an argument rather than a mere spectator to an argument meant for someone else. Second, it gives you the opportunity to act as a rhetorical critic who represents an intelligent reader's perspective on an argument that is important at this moment—an argument about pressing concerns for smart, well-informed college students and the people who care about them. When you analyze an argument as a secondary audience, you look carefully at the text, breaking it apart into its purposes and strategies and effects, and pass a judgment on whether or not such an argument should win our adherence. You take on the role of Representative Reader. By so doing, you also help us, your readers, understand more about how rhetoric works. I hope this perspective reminds you of our conversation in the previous chapter about the ethics of public discourse.

What an analysis might look like. You might be antsy at this point to see what an argument analysis looks like in writing. As your instructor will surely point out, there are many ways to analyze an argument because there are so many strategies for making one. In later chapters, you will learn about rhetorical appeals, stylistic tropes and figures, and other strategies writers might use to make arguments. There may be even too many to count—you have quite a toolbox as a rhetorical critic. (To see the whole "forest of rhetoric," check out Gideon Burton's resource at rhetoric.byu.edu.) For our purposes here, I'd like to show you what an argument analysis might look like based on the principles we've talked about in the last couple of chapters—claims, reasons, and assumptions. You'll notice that as a rhetorical critic, you'll need to make your own assumptions about how certain audiences respond to rhetorical strategies; that's part and parcel of the creativity that goes into analysis.

The following analysis is based on the Fleming article on NCAA wrestling. It's not a full essay, but I hope it gives you the flavor of what an argument analysis might look like.

> In "Wrestling's Dirty Little Secret," David Fleming makes a compelling argument that the National Collegiate Athletics Association should be held responsible when college wrestlers die trying to lose weight for competition. This quality argument (essentially, NCAA = bad!) is supported by reasons ranging from Fleming's own personal experience as a wrestler at Miami University to the vivid death of Jeff Reese, a University of Michigan wrestler who died "crawling to the [weight] scale" in the school gym. While

these reasons make his argument emotionally powerful, I suggest that they are not as strong as the reason Fleming gives as he concludes his provocative essay: The NCAA should be condemned because it *could* do something to prevent these deaths but doesn't.

The NCAA is a powerful governing organization. Fleming knows that. He also knows that while the NCAA "strongly recommends" prohibitions on body-torturing weight-loss practices in college wrestling, it tends to turn a blind eye to such practices—and student athletes suffer, and sometimes die, because of the inattention. Further driving this point home, Fleming offers several effective policies the NCAA could, in fact, implement, like banning plastic suit work-outs or requiring programs to do body fat calibrations to save lives in the future. The unspoken assumption is clear as a bell. Powerful organizations, responsible for the health and well being of others, should be blasted when they do not do what is easily in their power to do to prevent suffering. Fleming's argument works in part because we feel a collective need to hold our public organizations accountable to certain ethical norms. The emotional power of the personal stories in this essay is given even more weight when he shows how one one such organization, the NCAA, has been derelict in its duties to protect athletes from harmful practices.

If you're ready to go to the next level for analyzing arguments, take a look at Gary Hatch's treatment of *logical fallacies* later in this book.

Whew. We've covered quite a bit of ground in the last two chapters. Let's recap:

Arguments are not fights: they're intellectual exchanges necessary for democracy. When we make and hear good arguments, our judgment about public issues can improve. Arguments have several parts: a *claim*, a *reason* to support that claim, an unspoken *assumption* that must be true for the reason to be sufficient, and unspoken *rebuttals* that challenge the argument. Arguments are *rhetorical*—that is, they depend for their strength on whether the audience accepts the reason and assumption. Arguments are *invented*, using the tools of classical rhetoric, like *topoi*. And finally, arguments are meant for particular audiences—that's what rhetoric is all about—but there are multiple audiences for arguments: Primary audiences are audiences for which the argument is immediately and directly intended; while secondary audiences are made up of anyone reading the text and anyone interested or concerned about the issue the text raises. When you read an argument you become its audience, even if you weren't the *immediately intended* audience. And when you analyze an argument, you act as an ideal reader, making your own argument to help improve the civic judgment of others who have a stake in the outcome of the argument. Hey, someone's gotta do it. And it might as well be you.

EXERCISES

1. My guess is that you don't go around wringing your hands about the United States debt ceiling. Who does, really? Well, some people do. The debt ceiling is a number representing the actual limit of money the U.S. government can borrow to do what it needs to do, like pay Medicare patients or build tanks. (Actually, the Government doesn't just borrow money; it sells bonds, but I think you get the point.) Anyway, during World War I, Congress created a debt ceiling or a limit on the total amount of bonds the Government could sell. But guess what? Sometimes the U.S. Government spends more than it should, and then it wants to borrow money beyond the debt ceiling limit to cover its costs. Congress can decide to raise the debt ceiling, but sometimes representatives don't want to raise it for political reasons. Here's the danger: If the Government can't pay its own bills because the debt ceiling forbids it, then the Government *defaults* on its financial obligations. If that happens, the credit rating of the United States plummets because nobody trusts the Government to pay its debts and more bad karma awaits.

After a fierce debate in Congress about the debt ceiling in 2011, journalist James Surowiecki argued in the *New Yorker* magazine that the United States should not even have a debt ceiling—that Congress should abolish it. (What kind of claim is that? Yep, it's a policy claim.) What reason did he provide for this claim? He actually provided nine, but let's analyze three. For each of the arguments below, try to articulate the assumption, and then talk to a classmate about whether that assumption is strong or weak and why. Then think of at least one rebuttal for each argument.

The United States Congress should abolish the debt ceiling because...

- "every other democratic country, with the exception of Denmark, does fine without one."

- "there's no debt limit in the Constitution."

- "its negative consequences (default, higher interest rates, financial turmoil) are disastrously out of proportion to the behavior it's trying to regulate."

How would you use GASCAP or other *topoi* to categorize the reasons provided? (The first one seems like analogy to me.)

2. A school of communication studies at a university has recently banned laptops from all their courses. When students asked why, the professors argued that students end up wasting class time surfing the web or playing around on Facebook. Let's say—for the sake of argument—that the reason is a *fact*: in other words, it's true that when students bring laptops to class, they spend a certain amount of time surfing the web or Facebooking. If you were a communication studies student, how would you challenge this argument? (Hint: Start by finding and categorizing the claim.)

3. Find an opinion editorial or other argumentative text. Who is the primary audience? Who is the secondary audience? What claims, reasons, and assumptions are at work? Are they convincing?

NOTES

NOTES

NOTES

Chapter 4

KAIROS AND RHETORICAL SITUATION

Gary Layne Hatch

INTRODUCTION

Students often study arguments apart from any social context. They are often presented with a collection of written arguments lined up like zoo animals removed from their native habitat. Consequently, many students fail to realize that arguments are all around them. They may fail to realize that arguments make up an important part of how they live, work, and study every day. Whenever we are engaged with ideas and reasons, we are arguing. Whenever someone else makes a claim on our opinions, beliefs, and values, we are arguing. But placing arguments in context includes more than simply identifying who is engaged in arguing—the speakers and listeners, or writers and readers. The context for arguing also includes the time, places, and circumstances (Bitzer, 1968). When you understand the complete context for an argument, you will be better able to make sense of the argument and respond effectively.

Writing that matters, including argumentative writing, responds to the needs of actual people in real situations. When you argue, you are part of a conversation made up of the members of a community who care about the issue you are discussing. Others may respond to your argument, inviting you in turn to reply to their response. This interaction between writers and readers is called a **rhetorical situation**. A rhetorical situation is defined by the elements in any act of communicating: the writer/speaker, the audience (reader/listener), the purpose, the subject or issue, and the occasion. Figure 1 shows the primary parts of the rhetorical situation: the writer, the reader, and the issue.

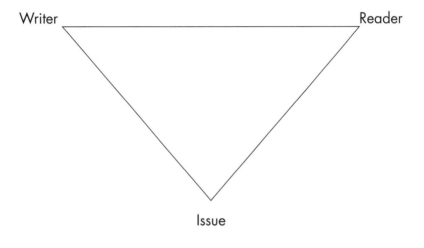

Figure 1

This interaction is mediated through symbols—language, of course, but visual symbols too. If you are in the position of the "writer," then you are making an argument through language or visual elements that addresses the issue under discussion. If you are the "reader," then you are trying to understand someone else's argument. In reality, we often take turns being the writer/speaker or the reader/listener.

A rhetorical situation is one that calls for the use of persuasion—it's a situation in which an argument would be an appropriate response. It's a significant moment that calls for a rhetorical response. Of course, because arguments are everywhere, rhetorical situations are everywhere too. Whenever true arguing occurs, it happens within the context of a rhetorical situation. Regardless of the reading or writing task, determining the rhetorical situation is key to understanding your role as a reader or writer. Understanding the rhetorical situation will help you define your purpose, audience, and subject much more clearly. And identifying your position in the rhetorical situation is essential to arguing effectively.

KAIROS AND KRONOS: TWO CONCEPTS OF TIME

Time is an essential element of rhetorical situations. Indeed, you could define the art of rhetoric as the art of knowing how to say the right thing to the right people at the right time. But what is the *right* time? The ancient Greeks had two concepts of time: *kronos* and *kairos*. **Kronos** is our typical concept of time, something that passes at a regular rate, measured in seconds, minutes, hours, or days. The word *kronos* persists in our English words *chronology* (the study of the passage of time) or *chronometer* (a device for measuring time—a fancy word for "clock"). To understand this kind of time, imagine a line extending to infinity in both directions (see Figure 2). The center of the line is the "present" and the arrows pointing in both directions represent the past and the future. This represents *kronos*.

Figure 2

Kairos presents a different concept of time, a concept based on the significance of the moment: it is "the opportune moment" or proper time to act. The Hebrew author of Ecclesiastes expresses this view of time in this famous passage:

> To every thing there is a season, and a time to every purpose under heaven. A time to be born, and a time to die; a time to plant, and a time to pluck up that which is planted; a time to kill, and a time to heal; a time to break down, and a time to build up; a time to weep, and a time to laugh; a time to mourn, and a time to dance; a time to cast away

stones, and a time to gather stones together; a time to embrace, and a time to refrain from embracing; a time to get,
and a time to lose; a time to keep, and a time to cast away; a
time to rend, and a time to sew; a time to keep silence, and
a time to speak; a time to love, and a time to hate; a time of
war, and a time of peace. (KJV 3:1–8)

Some moments in time are fraught with significance. Other
moments in time pass without much notice. Just as time seems
to move at a different rate when our attention is engaged
("time flies when you're having fun"), so some moments are
more memorable than others because of their significance to
us. One generation of Americans can remember where they
were and what they were doing when they heard that President
John F. Kennedy had been shot. Another generation remem-
bers vividly watching the space shuttle Challenger explode on
live television. Most Americans remember the morning of September 11, 2001. People remember the day they were married,
the birth of a child, the death of a friend or family member,
their graduation from high school or their first day on a new
job. Unlike other days, these moments were full of significance,
and as a result, these moments stand out in the flow of time.
They are moments of *kairos* in the flow of *kronos*.

THE RIGHT PEOPLE UNDER THE RIGHT CIRCUMSTANCES

As may be evident from the examples I just provided, *kairos* is
really about more than just the right time. *Kairos* refers to any
moment that is somehow a critical juncture of time, space, and
action. It's the right people at the right place at the right time
and under the right circumstances. These critical moments can
take different forms. They may be regular meetings, such as
town council meetings, court sessions, public hearings, stockholders' meetings, church meetings or committee meetings.
These may be ceremonies or rituals, such as weddings, funerals, graduations, or birthdays. One kind of action that critical
moments such as these can call forth is communication. For
example, guests at a wedding may toast the newlyweds. Graduation ceremonies and funerals have speakers. Proclaiming a new

national monument, winning or losing an election, announcing a new tax plan all require a suitable rhetoric—saying the right thing to the right people under the right circumstances.

A rhetorical situation brings members of a community together to discuss a particular issue, but the issue and the relationships among the participants in the conversation make sense only if you can identify the community or communities that these participants belong to. The word *community* comes from the Latin word *communis*, which means "shared" or "common." In its broadest sense, *community* describes a group of people who have something in common. Communities may be defined by geographical location or may consist of people who have a shared history, language, or culture. Communities may be formed by those who share the same social or business interests or the same political or religious views. Academic disciplines, departments in a college or university, and scholarly organizations often define themselves according to a common body of knowledge or domain of study, or shared methods of inquiry.

Communities overlap and intersect in a lot of interesting ways. Communities formed by shared interests or beliefs may transcend geographical boundaries, and a geographical community may contain many smaller communities defined by a common language or culture. And people may claim membership in a lot of different communities. For example, members of your class (one community) may belong to a variety of other communities according to where they come from, where they currently live, where they attend church, what social events they participate in, what campus clubs they have joined, or who they associate with. Even though you and your classmates form one type of community (your class), you would no doubt interact with each other in a different way in a different community— if, for example, you met at a sporting event or a political rally. We all belong to different communities, but we also share our membership in communities with others. Identifying ourselves with our different communities gives us our diversity, but because this membership is based on commonalities and shared beliefs and values, membership in communities also unites us.

DISCOURSE COMMUNITIES

One element of community that unites us is language. Nearly all people who interact with one another in a community do so through a common language. This common language helps to define any community because language initiates us into the world of a community and allows us to participate through the power of communication. (Notice that the word *communication* has the same Latin root as *community*. By its nature, language allows us to "share.") As members of a community, we learn the common names for people, places, objects, actions, and emotions. Through the language of the community, we receive the community's common values and beliefs. Another name for this shared language is "discourse," and a community defined by language is often called a **discourse community**.

A university or college is a discourse community. The boundaries of the college community are not only defined by the geographic space and physical barriers of the campus but also by language. Terms from the college discourse community include, among many others, "associate professor," "credit hour," "add/drop," "general education," "syllabus," "final exam," and "quad." Some first-time college students struggle with this language, and this struggle is part of what identifies them as newcomers to more experienced members of the community. Often no one bothers to define these terms for newcomers because more experienced members of the community have forgotten that there was a time when the terms weren't familiar. The problem of learning the discourse of the college community is compounded by the fact that the larger university is made up of many smaller discourse communities defined by separate disciplines, departments, majors, and fields of study. For example, the discourse of the humanities is quite different from the discourse of the social sciences or physical and biological sciences. If you study art history, for instance, you learn the names of the formal elements of art, the names of significant artistic movements, key figures in the history of art, and ways of interpreting and evaluating art. You would also learn ways of understanding art works within their own time period as well as examining the significance of the work within our own time. If you studied evolutionary biology, however, you would learn a very different discourse, the language of theoretical and experimental sciences, closely tied to the language of mathematics.

The campus community also overlaps with other communities defined by a diversity of cultures, religions, political views, and shared interests. Students on a typical college campus come from all over the United States and many parts of the world. They bring with them a unique mix of the communities that they identify with. Understanding that you are part of these various communities is important to help you know who the "right people" are to address in a particular rhetorical situation. Who you need to talk to depends on the shared language, beliefs, and values that define the community you belong to.

THE ORGANIZATION OF COMMUNITIES

Every community has a structure, an organization of power, a hierarchy of positions and roles taken by individuals within the community. The structure of the community can be fairly simple, or very complex, as with a government body or corporation, which may have organizations within organizations. There may be a formal, recognized structure as well as an "unofficial" structure behind the official one, a "shadow" organization. Considerable power, for example, may lie in the hands of staff or support people who work behind the scenes.

The university or college community that you belong to as a student is a complex organization, an organization made up of many smaller organizations. The structures of these organizations may overlap, often in confusing ways. Beginning students are often frustrated because they don't understand who to go to for help with a problem, who has the power to make and enforce decisions, or who they can talk to when they have questions. For example, what would you do if you became ill during finals week and couldn't take your exams? Most colleges have a well-established system for dealing with just such emergencies. You could usually contact your teachers or talk to someone in the departments that offer the courses you are taking. You could then request an "incomplete," a grade that allows you to complete the work for the course at a later time.

But even though this procedure is well known to faculty and administrators at the university, it probably isn't well known to students. How would students know about such a policy? It's usually contained in the policies section of a university catalog, but few students read this from cover to cover. But to be successful as a student, you need to learn how the system works.

Understanding the structure of the community—its distribution of power, its processes for communication and decision making—is an essential part of living in any community. Persuasive power can come from knowing how to say something that matters to the people that matter. But who are these people? And how can you get access to them?

For questions of public policy, the people who matter are those who have the power to make a change. These are the decision makers. Not everyone in a particular community has equal power or access to the political process. For example, you can debate an important social issue with your friends around the lunch table, but this debate probably won't have as much of an impact on the life of the community as it would if you could somehow present your views to a member of Congress, a lobbyist, or an influential member of the media. Although you can contact your Congressional representative, you probably wouldn't have the same influence as someone who can visit the representative face to face or hire an expensive team of lobbyists.

People who matter are also those who can give you access to conversations in the community, those who can help you to make your voice heard. Lawyers, for example, have greater access to the courts than do ordinary citizens. Newspapers and magazines have editors and publishers who decide which voices are heard in these publications. Television and radio stations have managers who decide what gets on the air. Even radio call-in programs, which appear to be very democratic, have a producer who decides which callers get on the air. Scarcity of time, space, and money limits the number of people who can join the conversation and how much they can contribute. Those who control access to the conversation are called "gatekeepers." To make a real difference, you need to know the process by which gatekeepers will allow access to meaningful conversations, and you will need to influence or gain the attention of these gatekeepers.

But just because you're not a decision maker or a gatekeeper doesn't mean you don't have influence. Understanding something about arguing, the organization of communities, and the nature of rhetorical situations may allow individuals greater access to power than they realize is possible. Sometimes a few letters to a member of Congress can influence his or her vote on an issue, particularly when the issue is not a highly publicized one. And although your influence may be small on national issues, you can wield considerable influence in your family, within your circle of friends, on your campus, or in your local community. The power of language also provides individuals with the power to organize, and in matters of public policy, there often truly is strength in numbers.

WHAT ARE THE RIGHT CIRCUMSTANCES?

Influencing people who can make a difference is not enough by itself. You have to address them under the right circumstances. For example, getting the right people in the right place is crucial. Discussions about issues important to a community take place in church buildings, courtrooms, boardrooms, student unions, and town halls. Nearly every university has a place on campus that is considered the "right place" to speak out on public issues (either by tradition or administrative decree). For example, at the University of Utah, there is a big rock near the Olpin Student Union that is defined as a "free-speech zone." At Arizona State University, people gather near the fountain in front of the student union or the lawn west of the library. Here they discuss politics and religion but also promote campus and club events. At Brigham Young University, students generally meet at "Brigham's Square," just outside the Wilkinson Student Center, where the university's student association occasionally sponsors a "soap box," an open microphone for students to speak out on issues of local concern. Colleges also have more formal spaces for discussion, such as classrooms, seminar rooms, or auditoriums. These have a different set of rules from, say, the fountain in front of the student union.

Time is also a consideration. Some occasions for arguing arise out of a particular crisis or moment of decision, but others are regularly scheduled in a community. City councils, courts, stockholders' meetings, and government hearings, for example, all follow a regular schedule for conducting their business. If you want to argue a local issue in front of the city council, you need to know both the place and time of the meeting and the process for getting your issue on the agenda.

Circumstances do make a difference. If you met the nine members of the Supreme Court at a party in Washington, D.C. and asked each his or her opinion on the landmark abortion-rights case *Roe v. Wade*, you wouldn't get an official Supreme Court opinion because although you have the right people, you would have them in the wrong place and at the wrong time.

THE LIFE CYCLE OF RHETORICAL SITUATIONS

To argue effectively, you need to know how to craft a suitable response to the right people under the right circumstances. Knowing how to do this requires that you know something about how rhetorical situations change over time. Such situations are not static; they evolve. How you respond to the situation depends on where it is in this process of development. Lloyd Bitzer, an important rhetorical theorist, calls the evolution of a rhetorical situation its "life cycle" (as cited in Hauser, 2002, p. 38).

In the earliest stages of this cycle, a need for debate exists, but the circumstances may not be clearly defined. Some people may not be aware of the issue or may not have organized themselves to respond to it. At this point, arguing can define the issue more clearly and raise awareness of the problem. As the situation evolves, it reaches a period of maturity where people are forming their opinions, arguing their positions, and beginning to make decisions. This time of maturity is *kairos*, the crucial moment to respond to the right people under the right circumstances. As this critical moment begins to pass, Bitzer explains that rhetorical situations enter a period of deterioration. At this stage, many people may already have formed their opinions, made their decisions, or begun to take action or implement plans. As people's opinions harden, it grows increasingly difficult for arguing to have an effect. Finally, the rhetorical situation enters a period of disintegration in which arguing can have little or no effect. Perhaps those who can make a difference have already made their decision or turned their attention to other matters. Perhaps plans are already completed or well under way (Hauser, 2002, pp. 38–40).

THE LIFE CYCLE OF A RHETORICAL SITUATION

Origin: The awareness of the issue is still forming, and the implications are unclear. Many people are unfamiliar with the issue or may not have strongly held opinions. The processes for discussing or deciding the issue are largely undetermined. Few groups may be involved in the process.

Maturity: The issues are more clearly defined, and processes for discussing and deciding the issue are in place. The moment of decision is approaching. Many different groups are engaged in the decision-making process. This is the critical moment (*kairos*).

Deterioration: The prime moment for influencing the opinion of decision makers has passed, and a solution may be in the early stages of implementation. Positions on the issues are well established.

Disintegration: The process of change becomes practically irreversible. Decisions have been made and put into action. Many groups have moved on to other issues.

Here is an example of the life cycle of a rhetorical situation. The state of Utah is considering building a freeway that would pass through wetlands near the shores of the Great Salt Lake. Proponents of this freeway believe it is needed to handle current levels of traffic as well as anticipated growth. Many environmentalists and some local residents fear that the freeway will destroy hundreds of acres of vital wetlands. In the early stages of this project, opponents of the freeway try to raise public awareness of the issue and of the importance of the wetlands and try to shape the process by which this issue will be discussed and decided. The primary approach here is to get the attention of the media gatekeepers and get the environmentalists' views on the public agenda. Once the process for discussing and deciding the issue is defined, the rhetorical situation reaches a point of maturity. All parties put forth their best arguments to the decision makers at the scheduled times and places. In this case, the state decides to hold a series of local hearings before debating the issue in legislative committee and making a decision. Those opposed to the freeway continue to raise public awareness and to persuade people to attend the hearings and make their voices heard (as do those who favor the freeway). When the process reaches the legislative stage, the environmental group works through lobbyists and tries to organize a letter-writing campaign for those legislators who are on the committee or who have influence on this issue. Once these hearings end and the committee makes its recommendation, the situation enters a period of deterioration. It becomes harder and harder to influence legislators and shape public opinion. After the vote is taken and the process of building the freeway begins, the rhetorical situation disintegrates, and the environmental group has to move to a new rhetorical situation, trying to get a court injunction against building the freeway.

DECORUM: A SUITABLE RESPONSE

Significant moments in time often require a fitting response. Special occasions may require that we dress or act in a certain way. A wedding dress, a graduation cap and gown, a Halloween costume, a judge's black robes, a soldier's dress uniform: all of these different ways of dressing indicate a recognition of what is appropriate or fitting for a particular occasion. Even when we go to a party or a dance, we dress a certain way, recognizing that these occasions are different from other occasions and require a different response. Acting in a way that is inappropriate for the situation shows a lack of decorum, for as one ancient Greek writer observes, "everything done at the right time is seemly and everything done at the wrong time is disgraceful" (as cited in Sprague, 2001, p. 283).

When you adapt your argument to the needs of an audience, you need to be careful to follow the conventions that guide the particular conversation you are joining. Each discourse community has its own rules governing what is "sayable," about what is understandable or acceptable. Generally, the more you conform to a community's conventions the more credibility you have with that community and the more persuasive you will be. You'll notice, for example, that when a political candidate addresses a particular group, he or she adapts to some of the conventions of that group. When addressing a group of college students, a candidate will usually dress down and try to identify with a younger crowd. As a candidate, Bill Clinton demonstrated this when he did his famous interview with MTV in 1994. He wore sunglasses and played the saxophone and answered questions about what kind of underwear he prefers (boxers or briefs?). When addressing a group of bankers, a candidate would dress in a suit and talk finance. When George W. Bush delivered his famous speech declaring the end to major combat operations in Iraq (the "mission accomplished" speech), he flew onto an aircraft carrier and emerged from the navy jet dressed in a pilot's jumpsuit. There isn't a guidebook to tell candidates how to dress and act when speaking before a particular group, but a successful candidate will find a way to "speak their language."

When you observe the workings of a community, pay attention not only to what people say, but also to how they say it. Saying the right thing in the right way is an art, and typically those who wield the most influence in a community have mastered it. You can develop your own sense of decorum by imitating those who are successful and finding a way to make their strategies your own.

DEFYING DECORUM

Although the best way to persuade others is to identify with them in some way, still there are some who are successful by doing just the opposite. Refusing to follow the conventions of a community, particularly if done in a dramatic way, can get the conversation going, redirect a conversation, or draw attention to an issue that might otherwise go unnoticed.

Those who challenge the community cause us to see the familiar in unfamiliar ways. They make the ordinary seem strange and new. They cause us to think about things that we would otherwise take for granted. We go through much of our lives without thinking much about what we do. Our experience becomes habitual and automatic. Think about some things you do every day—driving the car, taking a shower, getting dressed, eating breakfast. You have probably developed some routines that have become so mechanical that you don't even have to think about what you're doing. We also tend to follow routines in our habitual ways of thinking. Such routines are efficient, but by following them, we can develop blind spots. Someone once observed that we have become like fish in a fish bowl: we don't notice the water because it surrounds us. Artists, philosophers, and writers may challenge our ways of seeing, thinking, and perceiving the world. Andy Warhol was able to draw our attention to something as ordinary as Campbell's soup cans by framing them as art, challenging our conventional beliefs about what counts as "art." Socrates challenged the conventional thinking of fifth-century Athens by asking questions, exposing those who made false claims to wisdom. Abraham Lincoln credited Harriet Beecher Stowe with starting the Civil War because of the way *Uncle Tom's Cabin* caused a nation to reconsider its attitudes toward slavery. Martin Luther King, Jr. changed how many people saw the Civil Rights Movement through his "Letter from Birmingham Jail." Political activists and protestors may defy traditional decorum in order to draw attention to an issue that might otherwise go unnoticed.

Those who defy decorum do so at great personal risk. Not all members of a community will welcome the challenge and may threaten or alienate those who do things differently. But those who challenge the traditions of the community can play an important role in maintaining its vitality by helping us out of the mental ruts we can fall into through habitual ways of thinking.

CONCLUSION: TAKING ACTION

Novelist Ernest Hemingway warned us, "Never mistake motion for action" (Cole, n.d., para. 2). As the rhetorical theorist Kenneth Burke explains, action is motion with a purpose (Burke, 1945, p. 14). If you trip and fall down the stairs, you are moving but not acting. For many people, life is motion rather than action. Things happen to them that seem beyond their control. They are caught up in the flow of time (*kronos*) and seem to be victims of circumstance. Of course, we can never entirely escape our circumstances, but those who understand the power of language to shape and respond to significant moments in time (*kairos*) can gain some power over their circumstances and expand their individual freedom and influence. They become agents—those who can act—rather than those who are acted upon. The key to being able to influence the world around you is being able to see the rhetorical nature of these situations, the interactions among writers, readers, issues, and circumstances. By doing this, you can learn to craft a fitting response to these situations.

REFERENCES

Bitzer, L. (1968). The rhetorical situation. *Philosophy and Rhetoric, 1*, 1–14.

Burke, K. (1945). *A grammar of motives.* Berkeley: University of California Press.

Cole, M. (n.d.). *Cole's quotables.* Retrieved June 5, 2006, from http://www.quotationspage.com/quote/3793.html

Hauser, G. (2002). *Introduction to rhetorical theory.* Long Grove, IL: Waveland.

Sprague, R. (2001). *The older sophists.* Indianapolis, IN: Hackett Publishing.

NOTES

NOTES

NOTES

Chapter 5

RHETORICAL PROOFS

Ethos, Pathos, and Logos

Gary Layne Hatch

INTRODUCTION

In his famous definition of rhetoric (included among those presented in Chapter 1), Aristotle (1991) defines rhetoric as "an ability, in each particular case, to see the available means of persuasion" (p. 36). Let's take a closer look at this definition. The Greek word that Aristotle uses for "ability" is *dynamis,* which means "ability, capacity, or faculty." This Greek word should be familiar as the root of such English words as *dynamic, dynamo,* or *dynamite.* What do these words all suggest? Something that is active, forceful, and powerful. So rhetoric is the *power* to be able to see, for any particular rhetorical situation, all of the possible ways of persuading someone. Thus, rhetoric can be seen as the art of discovering possibilities. Which of these possibilities you choose depends on your particular rhetorical situation.

The Greek word that Aristotle uses to describe "means of persuasion" is *pisteis,* a word often translated as "proof," but this word also means "conviction, belief, trust, evidence, or assurance." This Greek word is the word used in the New Testament for "faith." So the "means of persuasion" or *pisteis* are the ways in which you build your audience's trust or faith in your message. What Aristotle describes are strategies that a speaker or writer could use to instill belief in others. This is particularly important in a situation where there isn't necessarily an absolute truth, where there is uncertainty or controversy. What strategies are likely to cause people to think more about a message to the point that they may actually change how they think about it? Aristotle describes three proofs: persuasion through a writer's credibility (**ethos**), persuasion through a reader's emotions (**pathos**), and persuasion through reasoning (**logos**).

ETHOS: ESTABLISHING CREDIBILITY

According to Aristotle, we are more likely to believe someone who is good. In fact, Aristotle calls one's character "the controlling factor in persuasion" (1991, p. 38). He uses the Greek word *ethos* to describe a persuasive strategy built on trust. This Greek word should be familiar as the root of the word *ethics*.

Think about people you trust. Why do you trust them? You might trust them because they have authority. For example, they may hold a certain position in the community. Religious leaders, teachers, police officers, and other public officials have authority because of the position they hold. The uniform, the badge, the sign of office are all persuasive in some contexts. Their authority can make them more credible. For instance, the President of the United States has certain authority because of his position—he can put ideas into action—and the office he holds conveys a certain degree of credibility on whomever holds the position. In the movie *The American President*, fictional president Andrew Shepherd describes the White House as "the single greatest home-court advantage in the modern world."

Others gain our trust, not because of the position they hold, but rather because of the qualities of character they demonstrate. Generally, we trust people who are knowledgeable and experienced, who are decent, fair, reliable, and honorable, and who demonstrate goodwill with others. We tend to trust people who are more like us, who identify with our values and beliefs. You might also trust someone because of his or her knowledge of an issue. Because we can't know everything about every issue we need to form an opinion on, we often value the opinion of experts. For instance, most people want to find a good doctor or dentist, one who is not only knowledgeable and skilled, but also honest and caring.

In a classic experiment conducted in 1951, social psychologists Carl Hovland and Walter Weiss did an experiment that showed the influence of credibility on persuasiveness. They gave two different groups of people the exact same written message arguing for the feasibility of building nuclear-powered submarines. One group was told that the argument was written by J. Robert Oppenheimer, a famous atomic physicist who had worked on the Manhattan Project (the project that developed the first atomic bomb). The second group was told that the argument was translated from *Pravda*, the official newspaper of the Soviet Communist party, widely regarded as a propaganda outlet for the Soviet Union. A large number of those who believed that the argument came from Oppenheimer changed their opinion, but very few did who believed that the argument came from *Pravda* (Aronson, 1999, p. 75). Similar experiments have shown what most of us would take to be obvious: "that a judge of a juvenile court is better than most people at swaying opinion about juvenile delinquency, that a famous poet and critic can sway opinion about the merits of a poem, and that a medical journal can sway opinion about whether or not antihistamines should be dispensed without a prescription" (Aronson, 1999, p. 75). What makes the difference here? Someone who is credible is seen as good, knowledgeable, and reliable.

Within the Catholic community, the Pope has credibility because of his position, and his credibility is enhanced by his well-known acts of service and devotion, his theological writings, and his years of experience in church leadership. When the Pope speaks or writes on religious issues, he can rely heavily on his position and reputation. Supreme Court justices also have considerable credibility by virtue of their position, education, and experience. Even though other members of the legal community may know as much as or even more than a Supreme Court justice about particular legal issues, a Supreme Court justice has considerable influence by virtue of having been appointed to the court.

But even those who hold positions of responsibility and influence need to rely to a certain degree on the art of rhetoric to be persuasive. Those who are relatively unknown must rely on these arts even more. For instance, because of their traditional role in the academic community, students are typically in a position where they may have limited credibility.

Consider, for example, the traditional research paper. Teachers expect students to include their own reflections and conclusions, but teachers also expect students to rely heavily on the opinions of experts and authorities. Students quote, paraphrase and summarize other writers, merging their voices with voices of authority to create credibility and show what they have learned about their topic. If a research paper came in with very few references, the teacher would probably be suspicious, perhaps wondering whether the student was guilty of plagiarism.

Teachers have different expectations for their fellow teachers and scholars. In an essay by an established scholar, a lot may be left unsaid because there is a body of common knowledge and assumptions about the topic that one has mastered as an expert. Established scholars rely much more upon their own authoritative voices and less upon the voices of others. Saying something that everyone else knows can label one as a beginner. Of course, experienced scholars still cite their sources, but the kind of sources they cite and the way in which they talk about their subject demonstrates that they are knowledgeable. For students to achieve this same kind of credibility, they also need to learn to talk about their subjects in a knowledgeable way. When a student opens an essay with a sweeping, panoramic introduction, beginning with "Throughout the ages . . . ," for example, or "In today's society . . . ," teachers may fault the student for overgeneralization or lack of support. But a famous historian can make sweeping claims about the course of history without a lot of specific detail and without always quoting the opinions of other historians. Ethos makes a difference.

There are some specific strategies that can increase a writer's credibility. Whether we want to or not, in every act of communication we give an impression of ourselves. The key in arguing is to be in control as much as possible of how we present ourselves. We manage credibility by presenting ourselves in the best possible way, establishing a relationship with our audience that is appropriate for the situation.

STRATEGIES FOR ESTABLISHING ETHOS

SHARING PERSONAL INFORMATION

Trust can come from what we know about a speaker or writer: his or her position or role in the community, prior behavior, and knowledge or expertise. When analyzing ethos in a written argument, the first step is to consider a writer's background. If you don't know much about the writer, then consider the background information he or she reveals. Look for stories the writer tells or examples the writer gives from his or her own life. Look for information about the author provided by an editor. You might even do some research to find out even more about the author. Then consider the following questions:

What is the writer's standing in the community?

What position does he or she hold?

What kind of authority and influence come with this position?

What is the writer's reputation?

What is the writer's education, experience, or expertise?

What about the writer's life is particularly appropriate for the issue under discussion?

As you construct your own arguments, ask these questions about yourself and consider what information about your own life might be appropriate to share with your readers.

ADOPTING AN AUTHORITATIVE VOICE

Writers can also establish credibility through the way they present themselves. For instance, it is important for a job applicant to make a good impression through a resume and in an interview. Even if an applicant has experience, education, and expertise, if these qualities do not come through on the resume or during the interview, then the candidate won't be hired. In other words, it isn't enough to actually *know* what you're talking about; you also have to *sound* like you know.

Writers can sound credible by adopting an authoritative voice. This includes properly using the language of authority for whatever issue we are discussing. We trust doctors, educators, and other experts in part because they sound like experts. They speak the language of science and education, languages that our society recognizes as authoritative. If you want to sound knowledgeable about science, you need to accurately use the language of science. Experts also know how to support their claims with well-documented, appropriate evidence. Studies, expert opinion, and statistics are not just an important part of a logical argument; citing them can also establish credibility.

Writers can also assume an authoritative voice through a technique called "voice merging" (Miller, 1992, p. 5). Voice merging occurs when a writer quotes, paraphrases, or alludes to an authoritative voice or to a voice that represents the values of the community. By merging his or her voice with this authoritative voice, the writer adds that credibility to his own. A political speaker, for example, might quote Thomas Jefferson, James Madison, George Washington, or some other political hero to lend authority to the argument. A religious leader might quote the Bible or some other sacred text. Some writers quote or allude to the works of literary figures considered great or important: William Shakespeare, Charles Dickens, Toni Morrison, or others. Citing such authorities is more than mere decoration; it also lends credibility to the writer.

IDENTIFYING WITH THE READER

When analyzing written arguments, consider how writers convey or create credibility by identifying with the values of the community. When politicians show themselves with their families, playing football with a group of marines, hiking the Grand Canyon, or visiting a school or homeless shelter, they are trying to show that they identify themselves with the values of the community. A writer does the same thing by using recognizable examples, sharing personal information, or appealing to reasons that support community values.

Choosing the right words is another way to identify with the reader. We trust those who "speak our language." One who speaks the language of the community seems to belong. For example, Martin Luther King, Jr., when addressing the African-American community, spoke the language of that community, drawing upon his experience and training as a folk preacher. But when he addressed liberal white audiences, a main source of support for his campaign for civil rights, he adapted his language, drawing upon his university training. In both instances, he strengthened his credibility by speaking the language of the people he was addressing (Miller, 1992, pp. 9–12).

SELECTING AN APPROPRIATE POINT OF VIEW

Point of view refers to the relationship the writer tries to establish with his or her readers. A first-person point of view (using "I" or "we") can create an intimate, personal, and friendly relationship between writer and readers, but "I" also draws attention to the writer as an individual. Doing so can be useful when a writer has particular expertise or relevant personal experience, or when he or she can speak as a representative member of a group. Using "I" may not be as effective, however, on formal occasions or when the personal experience of the writer may appear irrelevant, limited, or biased. Some teachers believe that the first-person point of view is never appropriate in academic writing, but in recent years, more and more academic authors are using "I" when sharing relevant personal information. Using "we" emphasizes what a writer shares with readers, but "we" can also alienate people who feel that they share very little with the writer. Readers might also reject a writer who seems to be overly intimate in order to draw them in, like avoiding a stranger who insists on giving them a hug.

A second-person point of view (using "you") immediately gains a reader's attention, as when someone calls your name out in a crowd or looks directly into your eyes. The second-person point of view is often used in giving instructions or warnings, and it lends itself very well to giving commands. Used too much, it can make a writer appear dictatorial, preachy, or condescending. Using "you" can also create a distance between the writer and reader or put readers on the defensive, particularly when they have some doubts about the writer's claims or motives.

A third-person point of view (using "he," "she," "it," "they," or "one") gives a sense of objectivity and formality. The third-person point of view creates a distance between the writer, the reader, and the issue, and it can give the impression that the writer is a detached and unbiased observer. For this reason, scientists and scholars often use the third-person point of view. However, the third-person point of view can make a writer appear apathetic and impassive. (Point of view and levels of formality are discussed further in Chapter 9.)

Giving a Balanced Presentation

Through their research social psychologists have discovered that we tend to trust someone who is apparently arguing against his or her own self-interest. Suppose, for example, that a convicted criminal was arguing that the judicial system is much too strict. Would you find that person credible? But what if that same person was arguing that the criminal justice system is much too lenient? By arguing that we should get tough on crime, the convicted criminal is arguing against his own apparent self-interest and for that reason may be more believable (Aronson, 1999, pp. 78–79). We also tend to be suspicious of people who are obviously trying to persuade us. A stockbroker who offers us a tip on a stock may just be trying to sell his or her services. But if we *overhear* that same stockbroker giving a tip to someone, we are more likely to believe the tip because it's not presented as part of a sales pitch (Aronson, 1999, pp. 80–81). This research suggests that if we want to have greater credibility, we should not give the impression that we are selling something or arguing in our own self-interest. One way to do this is to make sure that we give a balanced presentation, that we make it clear to the reader that we have considered and fairly presented all positions on a topic.

FALLACIES OF ETHOS

A **fallacy** is an argument that seems reasonable but isn't, an argument that is deceptive or manipulative in some way. Fallacies of ethos work in two ways. In the first case, a person misuses ethos by misrepresenting his or her authority. In this case, an author might try to win the trust of an audience by presenting himself or herself as knowledgeable, trustworthy, or interested, when in reality he or she is just trying to take advantage of the audience's trust. In the second case, an author might attack an individual who really is credible in order to destroy that individual's authority.

Ad Hominem

The Latin phrase *ad hominem* means "to the person." This term refers to a personal attack that has nothing to do with the argument. Of course, questioning a person's character or credibility is not necessarily fallacious. It becomes so when the attack on a person's character is used as a distraction from the real issue. For instance, it would not be fallacious to attack a scientist's experimental results if you had reason to believe that he or she had falsified data. An attack would be fallacious, however, if you based your criticism on the fact that the scientist had a string of outstanding parking tickets.

Some politicians use personal attacks as part of their campaign strategy. This is called "negative campaigning" or "mudslinging." A politician may rake up an opponent's past behavior, even things the opponent did when he or she was quite young, looking for anything that might damage the opponent's public image. Sometimes, politicians will even point to the irresponsible behavior of an opponent's relatives (siblings, children, in-laws, cousins) as a way of attacking the candidate's current credibility. But such attacks have little to do with the candidate's actual qualifications.

Guilt by Association

Guilt by association is an attack on an individual's credibility based upon that individual's association with a particular group. This fallacy usually works in this way. You generalize from the behavior of some members of the group to the group as a whole, stereotyping all members of the group, and then you identify the individual you are attacking with that group. Racial stereotyping is one type of guilt by association. For instance, a neighbor said he didn't like the fact that an Asian family had moved into our neighborhood because he had worked with some Chinese people and found them untrustworthy. He assumed that because he didn't trust some Chinese people, he couldn't trust anyone Chinese. He also assumed that anyone with Asian features must be Chinese. (This particular family was Laotian.)

POISONING THE WELL

A writer who "poisons the well" presents an argument in such a biased or emotional way that it is difficult for an opponent to respond without looking dishonest or immoral. This strategy is also meant as a distraction from the real issue and may involve personal attacks. Here's an example: "Of course, this liar will tell you that he didn't steal my stuff. You can't believe a thief. Go ahead and ask him; he'll deny it." How is the accused supposed to respond? The very act of asserting innocence in this case can be construed as a sign of guilt. The emotional and manipulative nature of the language in this case is a distraction from the real issue: who is guilty of stealing?

FALSE AUTHORITY

The fallacy of false authority occurs when an author tries to establish credibility without any real authority or when an audience is willing to listen to a person who is popular rather than one who is knowledgeable. Con men use the fallacy of false authority to trick people out of their money. Advertisements may also use false authorities, often by using celebrities to endorse various products. A basketball player may be an expert on athletic shoes, but is an athlete any more qualified than any other sweaty person to endorse deodorant? Does playing a doctor on a daytime soap opera qualify someone to endorse a particular medical product or service? Just because someone is an expert in one area doesn't make that person an expert in another. Having a Ph.D. in chemistry doesn't necessarily make you an expert on educational issues.

PATHOS: APPEALS TO EMOTION

In addition to gaining someone's trust, influencing your readers' emotions is also a powerful means of persuasion. Aristotle uses the Greek word *pathos*, which means "emotion," to describe a strategy of persuasion that appeals to the emotions. Overwhelming evidence from research shows that people are more likely to be persuaded if they are moved by a strong emotion, such as fear (Aronson, 1999, p. 85). In fact, although it isn't conclusive, there is some research that suggests that a message that is *primarily* emotional is more persuasive than a message that is *primarily* logical (Aronson, 1999, p. 84). This research suggests that even arguments that focus on logic will be more persuasive if they contain an emotional dimension. A logical argument may be convincing, but it won't usually be compelling. People may change their minds because of a logical argument, but pathos is more likely to cause them to change their behavior.

Although the Greek word *pathos* is the root for the English words *pathetic, empathy,* and *sympathy,* pathos concerns a much wider range of emotions than pity. In his *Art of Rhetoric,* Aristotle (1991) discusses anger and mildness; friendship and enmity; fear and boldness; shame and shamelessness; gratitude; pity and indignation; envy and emulation (pp. 122–162). A skillful writer can use fear, anger, humor, or compassion to put audience members in a particular emotional state such that they would receive a message that they might otherwise reject. Emotions literally put you in another state of mind. When people are afraid or in love, they may act in a way that to others might seem irrational. Because emotional arguments carry such power, you need to be careful how you use them and wary of how others may use them on you. As you analyze an author's appeal to emotions or when you find yourself responding emotionally to an argument, consider whether the emotions you are feeling are consistent with the issue and appropriate for the magnitude of the problem. As you compose your own arguments, you need to be responsible in how you appeal to others' emotions.

Emotional arguments can be found throughout an argument, but the direct emotional appeal is often stated near the beginning or the end. Placed at the beginning of an essay, an emotional argument can catch readers' interest and predispose them to read the argument with a favorable attitude. Placed at the end, an emotional appeal may move readers to action. Research suggests that strong emotion can be debilitating unless people are given some specific things they can do (Aronson, 1999, p. 87), so it would be appropriate at the end of an emotional argument to give readers something specific they can do to act on the emotion, such as a phone number they can call or website they can visit to register their opinion.

In most academic writing, the appeal to emotions is considered less convincing than ethos or logos, particularly when the appeal is exaggerated or manipulative. The academic community usually expects that any appeal to emotions will be used to reinforce a logical argument.

STRATEGIES FOR CREATING EMOTIONAL APPEAL

USING CONCRETE EXAMPLES

Concrete examples give an argument presence; they make an argument real and immediate for readers. Journalists recognize that running a photograph along with a news story makes the story more immediate. Showing a picture of a young child who has been kidnapped will create a much greater emotional response than merely reporting the child's kidnapping. Providing personal information about the child, showing her toys and family, or interviewing her classmates heightens the emotional response. A news story may contain statistics on how many families lack adequate food, shelter, or clothing, but few may respond. But if a reporter describes the plight of one particular family, then readers are more likely to help.

The emotional response created by a concrete example may make the difference between action and inaction. For example, on September 11, 2001, the nation watched in horror as a terrorist attack destroyed the twin towers of the World Trade Center in New York City, killing almost 3,000 people, including over 300 firefighters. The horror and emotion of the event were captured in Charles Porter's photo of firefighters carrying the limp body of Father Mychal Judge, chaplain of the New York City Fire Department, from the scene of devastation. This picture, and others like it, touched an emotional chord in the

American people because it put a human face on the tragedy, causing an outpouring of grief and sympathy.

Research by social psychologists shows that one powerful example can be much more persuasive than statistics. Even though studies and statistics may show that the Volvo is one of the safest and most reliable cars on the road, if your friend's cousin had a bad experience with a Volvo, you probably won't buy one. Even if a thousand people reported that they were satisfied with the Volvo, this one counterexample will carry more weight (Aronson, 1999, p. 90).

And the more vivid the example, the more persuasive it will be. Eliot Aronson (1999) conducted an experiment in which he worked with home auditors from utility companies to persuade consumers to add weather stripping to their homes to make their homes more energy efficient. One group offered statistics on the benefits of these improvements and met with little success. Only about 15 percent of homeowners agreed to make the improvements. A second group used a vivid example, explaining to homeowners that if they added up all of the cracks around all the doors and windows in their home, it would be the same as a hole in their exterior wall the size of a basketball. By using this example, auditors were able to convince 61 percent of homeowners to install weather stripping. This one vivid example made the difference (pp. 90–91).

Vivid examples come from vivid language. Instead of just telling readers how they should feel, writers try to re-create an emotional experience in such a way that readers actually do feel the associated emotion.

WORD CHOICE

Word choice is also important in creating an emotional response. Some words carry more emotional weight than others. Writers need to pay particular attention to the connotations of words, their suggested or implied meanings, in addition to the denotative or dictionary meanings (see Chapter 6). For instance, the words *cheap* and *inexpensive* both have similar denotative meanings. They both refer to something that can be bought at a lower price than expected. However, *cheap* can carry a negative connotation of "lower quality" as well as "lower price." To say that a person is "cheap" means that he or she is careful with money but with the negative connotation of "miserly" or "stingy." More positive words with roughly the same denotation are "frugal" or "thrifty."

Some words carry such powerful emotional overtones that they color other terms that are associated with them. Richard Weaver (1985), a political philosopher, literary critic, and rhetorical theorist, calls such terms "ultimate terms" (pp. 211–212). These are highly emotional terms around which other terms cluster. Ultimate terms with a positive connotation Weaver calls "god terms" (1985, p. 212). Those with a negative connotation are called "devil terms" (1985, p. 222). For instance, in the 1950s and 1960s, *communism* was a devil term for many Americans. Anything or anyone associated with communism—even obliquely—was painted by anti-communists with the same broad brush. In the 1950s, at the height of the anti-communist crusade by Republican Senator Joseph McCarthy of Wisconsin, even the slightest association of a person with communism or left-wing politics could ruin that person's life. For more obvious reasons, the word *Nazi* is another example of a devil term. In our own time, *terrorism* has become a devil term. The following words would be god terms for many Americans: *democracy, liberty, family, prosperity.* When you analyze emotional language in an argument, check to see if these emotional words form a pattern or cluster of related terms that may be connected to an ultimate term, either a god term or a devil term.

Writers should also pay close attention to figurative language, such as metaphor, simile, analogy, allusion, imagery, hyperbole, understatement, personification, rhetorical questions, and irony, all of which are discussed in detail in Chapter 6. Figures of speech draw attention to themselves because they deviate from the expected. For instance, an environmental activist might refer to the clear-cutting of timber as the "rape of the earth." *Rape* is a highly emotional term with seriously negative connotations. It suggests violence and domination. Readers would have difficulty responding positively to a word such as *rape.* At the same time, the word *rape* is used metaphorically, and the comparison of clear-cutting with the act of rape is obviously meant to shock. The comparison is likewise an example of personification because rape is an attack by one person on another. Presenting the earth as a woman in this way may gain the unconscious sympathy of readers who feel for the victims of sexual violence. On the other side, supporters of clear-cutting might refer to this act as "harvesting," using a word that carries much more benign connotations. *Harvesting* suggests farming and gaining the benefits of one's own labors. It may also evoke the nostalgia and respect that many Americans have for the traditional farmer.

FALLACIES OF PATHOS

Emotions play an important role in persuasion, particularly in moving people to act on their convictions. But emotions can be easily manipulated as well. **Fallacies of pathos** occur when an author uses emotions to obscure an issue, divert attention away from the real issue, lead others into errors in reasoning, or exaggerate the significance of an issue. Teachers, for example, occasionally hear fallacious appeals to emotion from their students. I once had a student who missed a lot of class and skipped some major assignments. He turned in a final essay, but it showed signs of being thrown together at the last minute. When I told him he wouldn't be passing the class, he complained about how angry his parents would be if he lost his scholarship. His implied argument was this: "You should give me a passing grade because my parents will be angry with me if you don't." The assumption here is that performance in college courses should be measured by how parents will react to the final grades. This assumption was unacceptable to me, but the student was hoping that the vividness of his emotional appeal would distract me from the flimsiness of the argument.

Ad Populum

The Latin phrase *ad populum* means "to the people." The term refers to a fallacious argument that appeals to popular prejudices. One of these is the *bandwagon appeal,* an appeal to popularity—if everyone else is doing it, it must be right. Here are a couple of examples: "It is all right for me to cheat on my taxes because everyone else does it"; "It's all right for me to break the speed limit because I'm just keeping up with the flow of traffic.

Besides, other people go faster than I do." The assumption in these arguments is that "just because something is popular or common practice, it must be right." Another ad populum fallacy is the *appeal to traditional wisdom*. This fallacy is an appeal to what has been done in the past: "That's just the way we've always done it." A related fallacy is the *appeal to provincialism*, the belief that the familiar is automatically superior to the unfamiliar: "That's just how it's done around here."

THREATS/REWARDS

The appeal to force is another name for a threat. A threat diverts attention from the real issue to the negative consequences of not accepting the argument. Extortion, blackmail, intimidation, hate speech, racial slurs, and sexual harassment are all examples of threats. The appeal to reward is just the opposite of a threat, diverting attention from the issue to what will be gained by accepting the point of view. Buying votes, trading favors, and bribery are all examples of the appeal to reward.

RED HERRING

The "red herring" fallacy probably takes its name from a trick once used by escaping prisoners: dragging a fish across their path of escape to throw dogs off the scent. A red herring is any attempt to draw attention away from the issue by raising irrelevant issues. This diversion often involves obscuring the issue with more emotional issues. Here is an example: "I don't think the president's economic plan is a good idea. I mean, what is he going to do about the violence in our inner cities?"

LOGOS: BUILDING LOGICAL ARGUMENTS

The Greek word *logos* has several different meanings. It can mean "word, thought, reason, or order." Our English word *logic* derives from *logos*, but logos has a broader meaning than logic. Logos refers to arguing through reasoning—the presentation of rational thought through language. Logos appeals to our ability to think; ethos and pathos typically work on our non-rational faculties, our abilities to trust and feel. Although ethos and pathos can be more compelling, logos provides the backbone of arguing, particularly for academic writing. Logos provides an overall framework of which ethos and pathos are a part. Arguments from ethos and pathos can be rationalized. In other words, they can be explained in terms of claims and reasons, but arguments from logos require claims and reasons as their basic structure. And although ethos and pathos are important to move people to action, it is logos that leads to conviction, to belief that lasts after the emotion passes. Logos protects us against illegitimate or manipulative uses of language and allows us to reflect on what we feel and what we believe. Although logos may not inspire people as much as ethos and pathos, logos will often prevent people from acting foolishly or rashly.

The power of reflection and contemplation associated with logos is what makes this appeal so important for academic writing. Academic authors typically value certainty, and they will usually approach conclusions tentatively until a preponderance of evidence convinces them that the conclusion is true or useful. This is why academic writers want to test one another's arguments and have their arguments tested by others. This is why scientists usually try to replicate the experiments of other scientists, why social scientists compare their data with the data of other social scientists, or why art critics will check an author's interpretation or evaluation of a work against their own. At its worst, academic argument can become as contentious and rancorous as any other argument. But at its best, academic argument leads to **critical thinking**, the ability to judge for ourselves the rightness of a claim based on the available evidence. Logos provides the key to this critical judgment.

When we supply reasons to support our opinions, we discover—perhaps for the first time—why we hold the opinions we do. We may also discover that some cherished opinions have no rational basis. In this way, logical argument and critical thinking not only create new knowledge, but they also can lead to self-knowledge, to a better understanding of who we are and what we believe. Critical thinking is part of the process of gaining an education. Through informed and responsible arguing, we recognize truths that would otherwise go unnoticed.

The process of testing ideas through logical argument is a particularly important part of a college education. According to the philosopher Richard Rorty (1999), a college serves two functions: providing students with "cultural literacy" and with "critical literacy" (pp. 114–126). **Cultural literacy** is an awareness of the common knowledge of the community of educated people. A degree in law or medicine, for example, certifies that the student who receives the degree has adequately learned the body of knowledge that scholars in the legal or medical communities value. But a university serves the additional function of teaching critical literacy. **Critical literacy** is the ability to question or explore what is believed to be true, to challenge or dispute the claims and opinions of others in an attempt to clarify and understand. Ideally, a college is a place where people can come together to ask questions, debate, and discuss ideas in a responsible fashion. This process of questioning and responding is critical thinking. It takes place primarily through language, through reading, writing, and speaking. Critical thinking can create tension, but it also represents the ideal for education.

STRATEGIES FOR CREATING LOGICAL APPEAL

So what makes a logical argument a good argument? Philosopher T. Edward Damer (2001) provides four criteria to use to evaluate arguments: **relevance**, **acceptability**, **sufficiency**, and **accountability** (pp. 23–31). These criteria are useful in analyzing arguments or in building your own.

RELEVANCE

First of all, an argument needs to be relevant. In other words, the reasons and assumptions offered need to relate to the issue being discussed. You can test the relevance of reasons and assumptions by asking yourself, "If these reasons and assumptions are true, would I be more or less likely to believe the truthfulness of the claims?" If you would be less likely to be convinced, then there is a good chance that the reasons are irrelevant. Testing the relevance of an argument is also a good way to check for manipulative uses of ethos and pathos (Damer, 2001, p. 24). If authority and emotion aren't really relevant to the argument, then you can set these aside and focus on the heart of the argument.

ACCEPTABILITY

In the process of analyzing arguments, you may begin to think that any claim can be called into question. In addition, reasons and assumptions can themselves become claims in need of additional support, leading to a chain of reasoning with no apparent solid intellectual ground upon which you can build with any certainty. Where does the justifying of claims, reasons, and assumptions come to an end? Couldn't a stubborn person keep asking for more and more support, disputing every statement in an argument, continually asking—as a young child does—"Why? Why? Why?" If one wants to be stubborn, yes; but such orneriness becomes ridiculous after a while. When arguments have a context, when they are a meaningful part of the life of a community, then at some point they can be grounded in what the community accepts as credible, authoritative, or true—the common sense or common knowledge of the community. This stock of knowledge differs from one community to another, and not all members of any group completely agree on what constitutes "common knowledge." This is why disagreements arise in the first place. But still there are statements and beliefs that most members of a community accept as true, and an argument will be persuasive only when the reasons and assumptions that justify the claim are grounded in the common beliefs of the community. Reasons that are grounded in the common beliefs of the community are called "community-based reasons."

One danger in relying on community-based reasons and adapting your argument to the needs of your audience is that you may compromise the integrity of your own views. In other words, you may end up just telling people what they want to hear. But it doesn't have to be this way. The reasons you choose to justify your argument may not be the most compelling reasons for you, but they may be the most convincing for those you are addressing. And if you can still accept these reasons, you preserve your integrity.

I once had a student writing an essay about a controversy in the small town she came from. A town ordinance forbade the consumption and sale of alcohol in city parks. Some citizens

wanted to change the ordinance to make the sale and consumption of alcohol legal by special permit. The intent of this
proposed change was to make it possible for the town to attract
concerts to the city parks, which many believed would help
the town's economy. At the same time, influential religious
groups in the town opposed the change because public drinking violated their religious beliefs or because they believed that
such easy access to alcohol would destroy the moral fiber of
the town, making it an unhealthy place to raise a family. These
groups argued that giving in on this drinking law would open
the door to all kinds of compromises in the name of economic
development.

The issue had polarized the town. Supporters of the change
saw members of the religious groups as being self-righteous and
judgmental or as trying to protect their own interests. When my
student wrote her discovery draft (her argument for herself),
she sided with those who objected to the proposed change on
religious and moral grounds. But she realized that because the
town was so polarized, these reasons might not be convincing to
the community as a whole or to the town council.

Being an emergency room nurse at the local hospital, which
was in a neighboring city that did allow the sale of alcohol for
park concerts, she knew that on concert nights the emergency room was overloaded with concert-goers who had had too
much to drink or had run into trouble with those who had.
Her own son even had to wait for emergency medical care on a
concert night. So in her next draft, she argued that allowing alcohol at concerts in her town—in addition to the neighboring
town—would overload the local medical system and ultimately
cost much more in human and monetary terms than it would
gain.

Even though this was not the most compelling reason for my
student, it was a reason that she nonetheless believed in strongly and one that added a new dimension to the debate, an argument centered in the common values of the community. After
all, who would deny the value of reliable medical care?

So how can you increase the probability that the reasons you offer will be acceptable to your audience? Damer (2001) suggests several ways:

- Build your argument on accepted common knowledge or shared beliefs and values.

- Draw upon your own experience and observation.

- Develop a chain of reasoning by building on the conclusions of other good arguments.

- Draw upon undisputed eyewitness testimony or expert opinion. (p. 26)

Sufficiency

According to Damer (2001), there aren't clear-cut guidelines for determining sufficiency. You just need to ensure that your argument has enough reasons and assumptions with enough weight to be convincing to your argument. As a general rule, anecdotal evidence is not enough. And a single example, although it may be vivid, usually isn't adequate to support a point. Because they can be tested by rigorous statistical methods, studies of various kinds usually provide strong support for an argument (p. 28). One way to ensure that you have sufficient evidence is to engage in a dialogue with others. Ask, "What kind of evidence or what amount of evidence would you require to accept this claim?" Determining sufficiency comes with experience and where there aren't established guidelines, it usually needs to be negotiated.

Accountability

I have used the term *accountability* to describe what Damer (2001) calls "the rebuttal principle." According to this principle, an argument should be able to offer an effective response to any other possible arguments (p. 29). In other words, an argument needs to be accountable to other perspectives, to counterarguments, and counterexamples. Some writers may think that by revealing to their readers other perspectives on an issue they may weaken their argument, but the opposite is true—if they can give a reasonable response to these other arguments. If you really can't answer other arguments, then perhaps it's time to reconsider your position.

FALLACIES OF LOGOS

Logical fallacies are arguments that look rational, fair, and valid, but aren't. If you take a logic class, you will learn a lot about formal fallacies—arguments that don't follow the proper form of a logical syllogism (see Chapter 2). The following are common informal fallacies: errors in reasoning related to claims, reasons, and assumptions.

BEGGING THE QUESTION

You "beg the question" when you offer a reason that is really just a restatement of the conclusion. For example, "You should exercise because it's good for you" is just another way of saying "You should exercise because you should exercise." That is, it begs readers to ask, "How is exercise good for me?" A writer also begs the question when he or she offers a conclusion without adequate support or uses reasons or assumptions that are just as controversial as the conclusion. Consider the following familiar argument: "Abortion is wrong because it is murder." This argument doesn't really advance the conversation about abortion because it offers as a reason one of the primary points of contention in the abortion issue: is a fetus really an individual human life that can be "murdered"?

COMPLEX QUESTION

A complex or "loaded" question is really two questions phrased as one. A famous example is "Have you stopped beating your wife?" The two questions phrased here as one are "Have you ever beaten your wife?" and "If so, have you stopped?" As the question is phrased, answering either "yes" or "no" will get a husband in trouble: "Yes (I used to beat her, but I stopped)"; "No (I still beat her)." Another famous example is this: "Are you aware that your tie clashes with your suit?" The introductory phrases "Are you aware . . ." or "Did you know . . ." usually signal a complex question.

EQUIVOCATION

Equivocation is using one term for two different definitions. When using this fallacy, an author will often have one definition in mind while allowing the audience to think that he or she means something else. When President Clinton was asked about his relationship with Monica Lewinsky, he insisted that he did not have "sexual relations" with "that woman." Many Americans accused him of equivocating in this case with the commonplace definition of "sexual relations" or the identity of "that woman."

HASTY GENERALIZATION/SWEEPING GENERALIZATION

A hasty generalization is another name for "jumping to conclusions." It is a conclusion formed on scant evidence. Here is an example: "They laid off five people at work today. That probably means the country is going into recession." The assumption in this argument is that a few people being laid off at one office is a sure sign of a coming recession. But the economy is so large and complex that five people being laid off at one office would have no effect. This conclusion requires more evidence.

A sweeping generalization is similar to a hasty generalization. It involves applying a statement that is true for one particular situation to another situation without considering how the two situations may differ. Here is an example: "My accounting degree really prepared me well for law school. Everyone who wants to go to law school should major in accounting." The assumption in this argument is that what is true for the writer is true for everyone. The argument ignores important differences among students. Some people feel well prepared for law school after studying English, political science, or philosophy.

FALSE ANALOGY

An analogy is a powerful persuasive tool because it presents an argument in interesting and memorable terms. Analogies provide the assumptions that ground many arguments. An analogy becomes fallacious, however, when the differences between the things compared are greater than the similarities. When the United States became involved in wars against communists in Korea and Vietnam, government leaders justified their actions by referring to the "domino theory." According to this theory, if communists were allowed to take over one country, neighboring countries would also fall to communism like a line of dominoes, risking world domination by communist nations. This analogy is a powerful and memorable image, but it ignores the fact that international politics is much more complex than stacking dominoes. The domino theory was also based on the assumption that Asian nations were like European nations in their politics and that one Asian nation (Korea) was pretty much like another (Vietnam). These assumptions proved to be false as well.

POST HOC

The full Latin name for this fallacy is *post hoc, ergo propter hoc,* a phrase that means "after this, therefore because of this." This fallacy refers to an error in reasoning based on the assumption that just because one event follows another, the first caused the second. A lot of superstitions originate in this fallacy. A person walks under a ladder and a bucket of paint falls on his head, so he tells people that walking under a ladder brings bad luck. The problem is that walking under the ladder didn't cause the bucket to fall (unless he bumped the ladder); further, to jump to the conclusion that there is a connection between ladders and bad luck is a hasty generalization. Buckets don't fall every time someone walks under a ladder. We just remember the times they do.

SLIPPERY SLOPE

The slippery slope is another fallacy of causality. It occurs when you argue that one event will inevitably lead through a series of related events resulting in disaster. It's found in the familiar warning given to kids: "If you steal a candy bar, then you will steal toys, then bikes, then cars, and then you'll find yourself on death row." It is true that most criminals started with petty crimes, but it isn't true that every kid who steals a candy bar will turn into a murderer. This argument is just designed to scare kids; logically, it doesn't work. The slippery slope fallacy is a favorite of political extremists who argue that voting for one candidate (or the other) will drive the country to ruin. It is true that voting has consequences, but a lot of other decisions would have to be made before an individual could ruin the government. You'll hear extremists argue that one particular bill, this one Supreme Court nominee, or just a slight increase in taxes will all bring the country to unavoidable disaster. Of course, fatal decisions can be made, but as with any causal argument, the writer should be prepared to explain exactly how the causal chain works.

Oversimplification

Oversimplification occurs when a writer makes an argument that reduces complex issues to a simple argument. An oversimplification may have some truth, but because it leaves out important information, it is misleading. Here is an example: "Jogging is good for you. Everybody ought to jog every day." It may be true—*all other things being equal*—that jogging is good for you, but some people may have conditions that make jogging harmful or inappropriate. One kind of oversimplification is *oversimplified cause*. This fallacy occurs when a writer tries to reduce a complex event or phenomenon to one simple cause, such as arguing that school violence is caused by video games. These may contribute to violence among *some* students, but a complex issue such as school violence can't be reduced to such a simple cause. Because causality typically involves complex relationships, the oversimplified cause is quite common.

Stacking the Deck

Gamblers "stack the deck" in their favor by arranging the cards so that they will win. Writers "stack the deck" by ignoring any evidence or arguments that don't support their position. For example, a drug company might stack the deck by releasing only the positive results of experiments on a new drug, suppressing any negative results. I once experienced "stacking the deck" when buying a used car. The person trying to sell me the car talked about how wonderful the car was. After I bought the car, the person trying to sell me an extended warranty pointed out all the things that could go wrong with the car. In both cases, these sales representatives were stacking the deck by ignoring either the good or bad qualities of the car. Whenever you're hearing only one side of a story, you should wonder what's being left out.

APPEAL TO IGNORANCE

The burden of supporting an argument falls on the person making it. A writer who makes an appeal to ignorance refuses to accept this burden of proof and tries to use the lack of evidence *as* evidence to support a claim. Here is an example: "Bigfoot, the Loch Ness monster, and extraterrestrials must really exist because no one has ever proved they don't." In fact, those who make the claim "Bigfoot exists" are the ones who need to support the claim. It would be a mistake, however, to assume that "Bigfoot doesn't exist" just because you don't have evidence that he does. "Bigfoot doesn't exist" is also a claim that requires support.

NON SEQUITUR

The Latin phrase *non sequitur* means "it does not follow." This refers to a conclusion that has no apparent connection to the reasons. Non sequiturs are often used in advertising. For example, a car may be pictured with a beautiful woman draped across the hood, the implied argument being "Look at this beautiful woman. You should buy this car." But there is no clear connection between the conclusion and the reason. The woman is just there to get your attention. It is not possible to identify a set of assumptions or reasons that would link the reason and conclusion in a sensible way.

FALSE DILEMMA

The false dilemma, or "either/or" fallacy, involves trying to force readers to accept a conclusion by presenting only two options, one of which is clearly more desirable than the other. Rarely are there only two positions on any issue. I have to admit, however, that my wife and I have used this strategy on our kids: "Do you want to get started on your homework or piano lessons first?" "Hard-sell" salespersons and negotiators often use the false dilemma to close a deal, to get people to say "yes": "Do you want to pay cash or credit for that?" (eliminating the option that you might not want to buy it at all); "If you don't act now, you'll never get another chance"; "Would you rather buy whole-life insurance or risk leaving your family without an income?"

STRAWPERSON

Imagine how much easier it would be to knock over a scarecrow than a real person. The strawperson is an oversimplified and distorted version of another's viewpoint that is easy to refute. A writer usually resorts to setting up a strawperson when his or her own arguments are not particularly convincing. In such a case, the writer has to weaken the other point of view to the point that it can be easily challenged. The strawperson works best when the other person is unable to respond or give a proper account of his or her own viewpoint.

CONCLUSION

As Aristotle makes clear in his definition of rhetoric, there is a power that comes from knowing how to identify and use means of persuasion. Once you learn what they are, you will see them in use all around you. Although there are many specific techniques for how to build credibility, create emotion, or build logical arguments, focusing on these broad strategies can make you a more effective communicator and help you to develop your own beliefs and values.

REFERENCES

Aristotle. (1991). *On rhetoric: A theory of civic discourse.* G.A. Kennedy (Ed. & Trans.), New York: Oxford University Press.

Aronson, E. (1999). *The social animal.* New York: Worth Publishers.

Damer, T. E. (2001). *Attacking faulty reasoning.* Belmont, CA: Wadsworth.

Miller, K. (1992). *Voice of deliverance: The language of Martin Luther King, Jr. and its sources.* New York: The Free Press.

Reiner, R. (Director). (1995). *The American president.* [Film]. United States: Castle Rock.

Rorty, R. (1999). *Philosophy and social hope.* London: Penguin.

Weaver, R. (1985). *The ethics of rhetoric.* Davis, CA: Hermagoras Press.

NOTES

NOTES

NOTES

Chapter 6

THE POWER OF THE WORD

Brett C. McInelly

INTRODUCTION

A few years ago while reading a student paper on the role sex education should play in public schools, I encountered a revealing statement. In documenting statistics regarding the percentage of young adults who have their first sexual experience during their high-school years, the student author writes, "By the time they reach high-school age, an average of 90% of the teenage boys have had sex, while 70% of the girls have lost their virginity" (Batchelor, 1994, p. 32). Although the percentages may be startling to some readers, I found the language the writer uses to be far more striking: boys "have" sex; girls "lose" their virginity! I suspect the student didn't think much about the distinction she was making in choosing to characterize in different terms the same event—the "first sexual encounter" for boys and girls. In fact, I wonder if the words weren't used unconsciously on the student's part. What the words reveal, however, are two very different attitudes regarding gender and sex. The first phrase is relatively positive—to "have" something is generally good—and indicates that boys are active; to "have" something suggests that one has taken possession of it. Girls, on the other hand, are portrayed as passive, since something (their virginity) is taken from them. The second phrase likewise portrays the first sexual experience as negative, since losing something is generally bad. While the student author probably didn't intentionally mean what the words imply, her language projects the idea that boys having sex is more acceptable than girls losing their virginity.

The student's word choice indicates something of the power of language: words reveal our attitudes, values, and perceptions of the world. While societal attitudes and values certainly change over time, it is fair to say that, historically, our society has had (and perhaps still does) a double standard regarding sex. Our culture has been much more accepting of sexually-active men than sexually-active women. In high school a sexually-active young man is often admired by his peers, whereas a sexually-active young woman is branded as "easy," perhaps even called a "slut." I wonder if this attitude doesn't carry into adulthood as well. What seems clear to me is the language the student author uses—to "have" and to "lose"—indicates this double standard, even if the student didn't consciously mean to suggest it. Her words reveal something of her and her culture's attitudes and values.

But language doesn't just provide a looking glass into our attitudes and values; it shapes those things as well. I would argue, in fact, that language even shapes our sense of reality. After all, the student author didn't coin the two phrases she uses to describe the first sexual experience for boys and girls. The words are ones she likely picked up in conversation, through the media, and in reading, and they've influenced the way she (and all of us) think and talk about sex. Consider, for example, what or whom you think of when you hear the word "virgin." I suspect that most of us immediately think of a female, perhaps one we imagine as pure and innocent; we generally don't think of an innocent young man. The word "virgin," then, influences the way we think about and the values we assign to women and sexual activity.

The point is that words both reveal and shape the way we look at the world, and this is important to understand when crafting an argument and deciding on what words will help us achieve a desired effect with our audience. If our goal is to influence, language is the principal means by which we will influence our audience. And since others are daily trying to influence us, we should be sensitive to the ways language works when analyzing arguments.

THE SOPHISTS

Early rhetoricians understood the power of words, and they spent a lot of time thinking about the nature of language and its effect on our perceptions of reality. In fifth-century Athens, a group of rhetoricians, known as sophists, focused much of their attention on the power of language and developed some of the earliest theories regarding the nature of language. One of their main motivations for studying the way language influences an audience resides in the fact that these men made their living by teaching rhetoric; sophists were teachers of argument. And they were in high demand, since being an active and influential citizen in Athenian society required a mastery of the rhetorical arts. In civic and legal life, individual citizens generally represented their own interests. There were no lawyers, so if someone brought a legal suit against you, you prepared and made your own defense. If you wanted to influence public policy, you made your case in the public square. To refine your rhetorical skills, you would likely solicit the services of a sophist to train you in how to make an effective argument.

While the sophists provided a needed service, they were not universally liked nor were their services always appreciated. Philosophers like Plato distrusted them, in part, because they believed the sophists taught their pupils to use rhetoric to manipulate audiences and distort the truth. From Plato's point of view, the sophists were less interested in the truth or facts of a case than they were in teaching people to win an argument at any cost. In short, Plato took a more idealistic view of things, whereas the sophists were a bit more pragmatic: for Plato absolute truth was the bottom line; for the sophists truth was relative or whatever you could convince your audience to believe. But both Plato and the sophists recognized that language has a powerful effect on audiences. As one fifth-century sophist explains, "Just as different drugs draw forth different humors from the body—some putting a stop to disease, others to life—so too with words: some cause pain, others joy, some strike fear, some stir the audience to boldness, some benumb and bewitch the soul with evil persuasion" (Gorgias, 2001, p. 32). Plato distrusted rhetoric because language could have this kind of effect; the sophists accepted the fact and sought out effective ways of influencing audiences.

Plato's trouble with the sophists partly explains why, historically, sophists have been given a bad rap. Curiously, the word "sophist" derives from the same root as the Greek words *sophos* and s*ophia*, which mean "wise" and "wisdom" respectively (Kerferd, 1981, p. 24). Hence, a sophist was originally one possessing wisdom. However, today the phrase "sophistry"—as in the statement, "That's just sophistry"—is used to describe confusing and illogical arguments, or linguistic trickery. And Plato was right to some extent: language can distort the truth and manipulate an audience. If people are using words in ways that seem dishonest or unethically calculating, we might (and probably should) call them on it. We also should avoid using language in such ways when making our own arguments. At the same time, we should be conscious of the lessons about language the sophists taught, recognizing that the words we use impact our attempts to influence an audience. We, of course, want to be responsible, but we should also be strategic in the words we choose to make a point. In most cases, the right word or words make or break an argument.

In short, whether as rhetors or auditors (i.e., one who reads/ hears an argument), we need to be aware of the nuances of language and understand that language both reveals and shapes perceptions of the world and of the issues we debate in public and private life. Developing this awareness involves understanding diction (or word choice), figurative language, and tone.

DICTION

When looking at diction, we need to recognize that words aren't neutral; that is, words aren't merely tools we use to communicate what we want to say. Although words certainly enable us to communicate with each other, we need to be attuned to the meaning that is implied in the words we choose to discuss particular matters or issues. We need to understand that a word can have a variety of meanings depending on the context in which it is used. For example, if my son, in referring to a passing automobile, exclaims to his best friend, "That's a killer car," his friend knows exactly what he means—that the car is especially stylish. If he were to make the same statement to his grandfather, his grandfather may not understand what he means by "killer." His grandfather might assume that the car is unsafe, either to the driver or to other drivers or pedestrians. This is because the word "killer" literally means someone or something that kills, but within the context of my son's statement, it means something else entirely.

This example illustrates what we mean by denotation and connotation. **Denotation** refers to the literal meaning of a word; **connotation** refers to all the other implications or associations we attach to a word. "Cool," for example, literally means moderately cold, but if my son had described the car by referring to it as "cool," he would have meant something similar to what he intended with the word "killer." Depending on how and in what situation a word is used, its meaning often varies.

Political pollsters, not unlike the ancient sophists, understand that the right word or words are essential to an effective argument, and they spend much of their time studying the ways voters respond to particular words and the meanings they affix to those words. They know that the words politicians use to frame their positions on particular issues are as important (if not more so) than the stance they take on those issues. One such pollster named Frank Luntz regularly conducts focus groups with voters to determine the associations people make with particular words in order to advise his clients—Republican politicians. In one such group, he asked a group of middle-class voters what they thought of when they heard the word "government." Their responses were revealing: "Controlling," "Bureaucracy," "Corruption," and "Liars." What Luntz discovered is that, in the minds of many voters, "government" has a negative connotation. Hence, he advises his clients to claim they are for "less government" and to accuse Democrats of wanting "more government" in American life (LeMann, 2000, pp. 104–105). Rather than refer to "global warming," he advises politicians to speak of "climate change." Why? Both phrases ostensibly describe the same phenomenon, but the second phrase is not nearly as threatening or ominous as the first; the first phrase has a much more negative connotation (LeMann, 2000, p. 100).

Part of Luntz's point is that words shape the way people think about and respond to particular issues. Luntz advises Republicans to talk about "tax relief" instead of "tax cuts" (LeMann, 2000, p. 100). In this case, "tax cuts" doesn't necessarily have a negative connotation; rather, "tax relief" frames the issue in such a way as to suggest that citizens are overburdened by taxes and in need of "relief." The phrase "tax relief" thus produces a stronger emotional response, since many Americans feel like they are overtaxed, and, from Luntz's point of view, the phrase is a more effective way of marshalling support for initiatives to reduce taxes. Luntz also found that many voters are more inclined to do away with a "death tax," whereas they were much more supportive of an "estate tax." Curiously, both phrases describe the same thing, so why is the former less appealing than the latter? The word "estate" is associated with wealth and prosperity; people tend to think that only the rich have "estates," and most middle-class voters aren't opposed to taxing the wealthy. "Death tax," on the other hand, sounds "unfair": "You work hard your whole life and the government takes it all away at the end" (LeMann, 2000, p. 105). What Luntz tries to get across to his clients is that the language they use to discuss issues shapes voters' perceptions and that getting elected or advancing public policy depends on a politician's rhetoric, not just his or her stance on the issues (LeMann, 2000, p. 109).

Luntz and others who provide this kind of advice have been criticized for what appears to some people as a manipulative way of using language to achieve political aims. Like the sophists, they're accused of disregarding the truth or facts of a situation, relying instead on linguistic tricks to represent an issue in the most politically advantageous way possible. These critics' accusations aren't entirely unfounded. Politicians certainly have been known to use language in deceptive ways. During his first presidential campaign in 1988, George Bush, Sr. made a statement that some analysts would later argue cost him the White House in 1992. In a speech at the Republican National

Convention, he said, "Read my lips: no new taxes." When taxes were raised during his presidency, Bush's critics charged him with lying to win the election. In his defense, Bush insisted that the government hadn't created "new" taxes but had merely raised existing ones. Democrats then accused Bush of equivocating—intentionally using one phrase with at least two different meanings—to win votes. When voters heard Bush claim there would be "no new taxes," they assumed taxes wouldn't be raised; when taxes were raised and Bush offered his defense, many citizens felt as if Bush had been intentionally deceptive.

Language thus can be used in questionable and potentially unethical ways, and we need to be aware of this when weighing the merits of an argument. When making arguments of our own, our aim hopefully isn't to mislead our audience or misrepresent the facts. At the same time, we need to recognize that an effective argument requires the right words as well as the right stuff or substance. The way our argument is perceived by an audience is strongly affected by our language and the associations readers make with the words we use. Consider, for example, the abortion debate. Those against abortion claim to be "pro-life"; those in favor of it claim to be "pro-choice." Both phrases ostensibly have a positive connotation. Who, after all, isn't an advocate for "life" or "choice?" Pro-life advocates certainly wouldn't say they are, at least in a general sense, opposed to the freedom to choose, and pro-choice advocates wouldn't say they're in favor of death or murder. Each group has chosen a phrase that frames their position in positive terms, and I don't think either phrase is intended to deliberately misrepresent the respective positions on the issue. Rather, they've chosen phrases that are rhetorically effective. This should be our goal when choosing the words to make our arguments.

FIGURATIVE LANGUAGE

Diction, then, is a powerful feature of an argument. So too is figurative language. Figurative language enables us to make our points in particularly memorable and meaningful ways. In a nutshell, **figurative language** involves using one thing or idea to represent another. Perhaps the most common example is the metaphor, which in the original Greek meant to "transfer."

Essentially, a **metaphor** is a comparison in which you "transfer" the meaning of one thing or object to another. For example, when Forrest Gump says, "Life is like a box of chocolates," he is using a **simile**, which is a type of metaphor using "like" or "as"; he is "transferring" the associations we make with eating a box of chocolates to life. By so doing, he is suggesting that life is unpredictable and full of surprises ("You never know what you're going to get").

So why not just say, "Life is full of surprises"? Why bother using a metaphor? In this particular case, I would argue that the metaphor is more memorable and makes the point more effectively because eating a box of chocolates is something most of us can relate to. Most of us have had the experience of choosing a chocolate. When surveying the box, all the chocolates look delicious, but we know from experience that not all the chocolates are equally satisfying to our own individual tastes. Sometimes we make a choice we are happy with; other times we are disappointed and wish we would have chosen a different one. Sometimes we don't get the one we had hoped for, but we are pleasantly surprised with the result. The point is we can never be sure of the outcome, but we have to make a choice nonetheless. According to Forrest, the experience of choosing a chocolate is a lot like the choices we make in life, and the metaphor is a particularly poignant way of making his point.

Let's consider a more elaborate metaphor. In the novel *A Farewell to Arms* by Ernest Hemingway, the main character finds himself sitting in a hospital waiting room at the end of the narrative. An ambulance driver in Italy during World War I, he has abandoned his post (hence, *A Farewell to Arms*) and run away to Switzerland with the woman he loves, a nurse. She has just delivered a stillborn baby and is about to die herself from complications associated with the delivery. As the main character recognizes that he has lost a child and will soon lose the woman he loves, he reflects on the nature of life and death. He has seen firsthand the brutality of war and human existence, and he eventually adopts a rather pessimistic worldview he describes in the following metaphor:

Once in camp I put a log on top of the fire and it was full of ants. As it commenced to burn, the ants swarmed out and went first toward the centre where the fire was; then turned back and ran toward the end. When there were enough on the end they fell off into the fire. Some got out, their bodies burnt and flattened, and went off not knowing where they were going. But most of them went toward the fire and then back toward the end and swarmed on the cool end and finally fell off into the fire. I remember thinking at the time that it was the end of the world and a splendid chance to be a messiah and lift the log off the fire and throw it out where the ants could get off onto the ground. But I did not do anything but throw a tin cup of water on the log, so that I would have the cup empty to put whiskey in before I added water to it. I think the cup of water on the burning log only steamed the ants. (pp. 327–328)

From the point of view of the main character, the experience of the ants parallels our own, in that we lead a harsh and seemingly senseless existence. If we survive, we do so only after experiencing great hardship and pain. This is certainly how the main character feels in the wake of losing his child and the woman he loves, to say nothing of the many friends he's seen die in battle. The experience of watching the ants on the log also reflects his thoughts regarding God. If a god does exist, the metaphor suggests that he looks on human suffering with little or no sympathy and does not intervene on our behalf. The metaphor of the ants on the log is thus an effective way for Hemingway to communicate to his readers a particular worldview and is certainly more effective than just saying that we live in a cruel and godless universe.

The metaphor is just one example of what is known as a figure of speech. In our language, there are literally hundreds of figures of speech, too many to be addressed comprehensively here. The important thing is to recognize when people are using language figuratively and to grasp the implications of a figure of speech. We also want to refine our ability to use figurative language in rhetorically effective ways. To assist you in recognizing and using figures of speech, here is a list of some of the more common figures, in addition to metaphor and simile, you will encounter in arguments.

Analogy: a kind of comparison in which something unfamiliar is explained by a comparison to something more familiar. In arguing that public-school curricula should include the study of religion, Warren A. Nord (2002) makes the following analogy: "For some time now, people have rightly argued that ignoring black history and women's literature (as texts and curricula have traditionally done) has been anything but neutral. Rather, it betrays a prejudice; it is discriminatory. And so it is with religion" (p. 174). Most people recognize that black history and the contributions of women to literature have not been given their due in public education, but most people do not recognize that, at least according to Nord, religion has been similarly marginalized.

Allusion: a reference to a historical event or person. Allusions are also made to events and persons from literature and other media (film, television, etc.). For example, Martin Luther King, Jr. begins his "I Have a Dream" speech with an allusion to Abraham Lincoln's "Gettysburg Address": "Five score years ago, a great American, in whose symbolic shadow we stand, signed the Emancipation Proclamation." In alluding to the opening of Lincoln's speech ("Four score and seven years ago . . .") King indirectly suggests that he is a modern-day Lincoln in his championing of civil rights while simultaneously paying homage to a revered American leader.

Imagery: particularly vivid language that evokes a mental image of what is being described. Imagery often encourages an emotional response. In decrying the practice of parents who withhold medical treatment from their children on religious grounds (Christian Science, for example, advocates faith healing in place of medical treatment), Rita Swan (2002) uses vivid imagery to portray the suffering of one child who died of bone cancer: "the tumor on her leg was more than forty inches in circumference and her genitalia were partially rotted away from lying in her own excrement" (p. 147).

Overstatement: also known as hyperbole, overstatement is the use of exaggeration to make a point. I have a friend who, upon entering a particularly chilly room, will exclaim, "You could store meat in here!" He is clearly exaggerating, but his statement effectively emphasizes how cold the room is.

Understatement: to state or represent something in terms that do not fully encapsulate its magnitude. If I accidentally touch a hot stove and my wife asks, "Was it hot?" I might respond by saying, "Just a bit," as I hurry to the freezer for an ice cube. By stating the opposite of what I mean, my wife understands exactly that the stove was, in fact, hot. As with overstatement, understatement can be an effective way to make a point.

Personification: giving human characteristics to animals, abstract ideas, and inanimate objects. As described in Chapter 5, referring to the clear-cutting of forests as a "rape of the earth" personifies the earth as a victim of violence.

Rhetorical Question: a stated question that does not necessitate a reply or answer. Such questions often have strong rhetorical effect. A politician mustering support for the War on Terror might string together a series of questions to rally support: "Don't all Americans want freedom? Don't we all want democracy? We can't have freedom or democracy until terrorism is a thing of the past."

Irony: saying one thing but meaning the opposite. In *A Modest Proposal*, the eighteenth-century author, Jonathan Swift, suggests that the Irish breed and then rear children, like cattle, for food for the English. Swift's intention isn't to encourage people to accept an outrageous proposal; rather, he hopes to draw attention through irony to English exploitation of the Irish. From his point of view, this exploitation is as bad or worse than his proposal.

DICTION AND FIGURATIVE LANGUAGE AT WORK IN AN ARGUMENT

To illustrate the ways figurative language, along with diction, work in an argument, let's look at a passage from an article drawing attention to the violent nature of the turtle-farming industry:

> Before being killed and canned, the turtles swim in dense kraals, bumping each other in the murky water, armor clashing, dully lurching against high pens. Later, trussed on a plank dock, they lie unblinking in the sun, their flippers pierced and tied. The tough leather of their skins does not disguise their present helplessness and pain. They wear thick, sun-hardened accumulations of blood at their wounds. Barbados turtles, as large as children, they belong to a species which has been eliminated locally by ardent harvesting off the waters near Key West, but the commercial tradition still brings them here to be slaughtered. Crucified like thieves, they breathe in little sighs, they gulp, they wait.
>
> At a further stage, in the room where the actual slaughtering occurs, the butchers stride through gore in heavy boots. The visitor must proceed on a catwalk; a misstep will plunge him into a slow river of entrails and blood. (Gold, 2002, p. 219)

You may have noticed the two similes—"as large as children" and "Crucified like thieves." The first is also an example of personification, humanizing the turtles and suggesting their helpless condition; the second emphasizes their pain, since most people understand that the Roman practice of crucifixion was an extremely agonizing form of execution. The reference to crucifixion also makes an allusion to Jesus Christ, since most people are aware that Christ was crucified. The implication here is that the turtles, like Christ, are innocent victims of the brutality of others. The imagery ("murky water," "dully lurching," "sun-hardened accumulations of blood," "a slow river of entrails and blood," etc.) enables the reader to visualize the horrific nature of the scene. These elements combine to create a strong emotional appeal (pathos).

The diction is likewise effective in establishing the passage's persuasive appeal. Note that the turtles are "killed," not harvested. "Killed," of course, has a negative connotation, emphasizing the brutality of the practice and the innocence of the turtles. And the workers are not "farmers"; they are "butchers." Of course, one meaning of "butcher" is one who cuts or processes meat, so the term is accurate. But within the context of the passage, it is intended to portray these workers as the perpetrators of the turtles' misery. They are essentially portrayed as callous murderers.

TONE

The written word often projects the mood or attitude of the writer toward the subject or the audience. This is what we mean by **tone**. Tone is also a characteristic or attribute of voice (see Chapter 9). When speaking, we project our mood or attitude through body language, inflections in our voice, and so forth. When writing, tone is primarily created through our word choice, and as with speaking, our mood or attitude can be characterized in a number of ways: formal or casual, serious or playful, earnest or sarcastic, reasonable or angry, and on and on. In other words, we can project the full range of human emotions and attitudes in the language we use to discuss a topic. Consider the following examples, the first from an argument in support of prayer in school and the other from Nord's argument for more accommodation of religion in public-school curricula:

> Has anyone ever heard a pregame prayer? I have. Used to hear them all the time, in the '50s, at Corsicana High School football games. Guess what they prayed for over the P.A. system? America's conversion to the regimen of the First Methodist Church? Not a chance. Rather, for a clean game, and for the safe return of all fans to their homes. Gosh! What dangerous stuff! Likely to result in the overthrow of civilization! (Murchison, 2002, pp. 191–192)

> In the current culture wars, religious liberals tend to ally themselves with the educational establishment against those on the Religious Right who are attacking the public schools. In politics and theology, I line up with the left.

Nonetheless, I believe with the right that public education is hostile to religion—not least to liberal education. (Nord, 2002, p. 170)

Both examples are written in the first-person ("I"), but the first passage is much more informal, using colloquial, conversational expressions (e.g., "Gosh!") to make the writer's point. The attitude of this writer toward the issue at hand is sarcastic, particularly evident in his use of overstatement ("What dangerous stuff! Likely to result in the overthrow of civilization!"). The second example is more formal and serious, though it is equally direct and assertive.

So which is the more effective approach? That depends on the writer's rhetorical situation. The first writer, Bill Murchison, is a syndicated columnist, which means he probably has a following—that is, readers who read his column regularly. These readers probably read his column because they enjoy his writing style or because they tend to agree with his viewpoint on particular issues. They expect Murchison's writing to be informal and have an edge to it. With this audience his tone is probably effective. Warren Nord, on the other hand, is a university professor and is writing for a publication that examines issues of politics, culture, and theology. Readers of this kind of magazine expect more formal and serious commentary on these issues. Given each writer's rhetorical situation, each has adopted a tone that is appropriate and effective for his respective purpose and audience.

And this is the point: our rhetorical situations should dictate the mood or attitude we project in our writing. In a letter in which we try to persuade a friend to accompany us on a vacation, we can probably afford to use a casual, even playful tone; when writing a paper for our psychology teacher on cognitive development, however, casual and playful would likely prove an inappropriate rhetorical choice on our part.

Perhaps a real-life example will help make my point here. Several years ago my wife and I were vacationing in Hawaii. Returning from a dinner cruise, we discovered that the car we had been driving had been ticketed for parking with the rear of the car facing a parking meter. I had backed into the stall and put ample change into the meter for the time we would be away from the car. Needless to say, we were surprised that we had been ticketed. Neither of us had ever heard of an ordinance in any city that prohibits parking with the rear of the car facing a parking meter. Even my in-laws, who lived in Hawaii at the time, didn't know that parking in such fashion was illegal. It was only after contacting the traffic bureau that we learned that Honolulu has such an ordinance. What made matters worse, the fine was $100!

My initial reaction to the ticket was anger. I felt like, as a tourist, I had been taken advantage of. While there may have been good reason for the ordinance, I believed the city had an obligation to post signs on the meters informing drivers of the ordinance, especially since many drivers in Honolulu are tourists and are probably unaware of those laws unique to the city. Given the unusual nature of the ordinance, it seemed like a tourist trap, since I'm sure I wasn't the first tourist to be ticketed for this same infraction. And the $100 fine seemed excessive, to say the least.

I decided to fight the ticket. To do so, I would have to write a letter to the judge, since my vacation ended before I could appear in court. In planning my argument, I had to decide the tone I wanted my letter to take. As I've mentioned, I was angry at the time. Part of me wanted to unload on the judge in the most aggressive language I could muster. I realized, however, that this probably wouldn't be the most effective rhetorical approach. I assumed the judge probably wouldn't respond well to an angry or sarcastic assault on his city and its driving ordinances. If my goal was to persuade him to dismiss the fine, I decided I would need to make a calm and reasonable argument. But I also wanted to be assertive. Here is a passage from my letter:

> Given the relatively unusual nature of the ordinance as well as the number of tourists who visit Honolulu, I am surprised that signs explaining the ordinance are not posted in metered parking lots. It seems unreasonable to assume that visitors to your city and state would be aware of such an ordinance, nor is it likely that tourists are going to consult

the kinds of publications that explain those laws unique
to Honolulu. It seems to me that your community has a
responsibility to better inform visitors of the kinds of ordinances I unknowingly violated.

I'll let you determine how successful I was in creating a calm
and reasonable tone. But just for fun, let's revise the passage so
it reflects the way I felt at the time I received the ticket:

Given the completely idiotic and senseless nature of the ordinance as well as the number of tourists who spend their
hard-earned money in Honolulu, I can't believe that signs
explaining this ridiculous ordinance aren't posted in me-
tered lots. Do you really expect tourists, people on vacation,
to take the time to read up on your driving ordinances? I
would suggest that you and your city start doing a better job
of informing people of your stupid laws.

While this second passage was fun to write, and perhaps more
accurately expresses how I felt, it certainly wouldn't have been
as rhetorically effective with my audience. (Incidentally, the
judge eventually dismissed my ticket.)

One final thing. You will notice when comparing the two passages above that tone can be altered dramatically by only a word
or two. Consider the different mood projected by referring to
the ordinance as "idiotic" as compared to "unusual." Hence,
whether creating tone or assessing someone else's tone, we
need to pay particular attention to diction and recognize the
options at our disposal. And we always need to be aware of the
rhetorical situation and assess the effectiveness and appropriateness of tone in relationship to our subject, our purpose, and
our audience.

CONCLUSION

Words ultimately make (or break) an argument. While we certainly need to attend to a variety of considerations when crafting an argument—rhetorical situation, our claims and use of
evidence, etc.—we need to pay equal attention to each and every word we use, every figure of speech, and our tone. We need
to realize that these features of our arguments go a long way

in shaping the way our readers perceive us and the issues we address. We can have all the evidence in the world supporting our position, but if our language doesn't work, neither will the argument. And as individuals who are daily bombarded with one argument after another, we need to attune ourselves to the ways language works to produce an effect. We need to realize that the words others use to persuade us aren't just sending a message; they are working to influence and shape the way we look at the world.

In short, we need to be more conscious of language and its effects. As writers, we need to consider all of our options when deciding on the language we use to make our points. For example, when writing my letter to the judge regarding my parking ticket, I considered several words I could use to describe the parking ordinance I had violated—"idiotic," "stupid," "ridiculous," "odd," "unusual," etc. I chose "unusual" because it seemed like the least offensive and projected the tone I was aiming for. At another place in the letter, I thought an analogy might help me more effectively make a point: "Having and enforcing this ordinance on visitors [who are unaware of it] is like asking someone to play a game and not telling them the rules, and then penalizing them the second they break the rules." My goal in using the analogy was to describe what I perceived as the unjust nature of the law and its enforcement, and I thought a figure of speech might help my audience better understand how I felt at the time.

The point is that my word choice, my use of figurative language, and my tone were issues I thought through as I planned and executed my argument. I left nothing to chance, especially my language. As you decide on what evidence to use to support a claim, or what types of appeals will be most effective—ethical, emotional, logical—you likewise need to consider the linguistic issues we've explored in this chapter to effectively influence your audience.

When analyzing an argument, we should probably highlight words that seem especially significant and consider the implications of those words. In the passage describing the turtle-farming industry, the word "killer" is especially significant, so

I chose to focus on it and the associations we attach to it when analyzing the passage. We should also note when arguments are using figures of speech and flesh out all the implications of a figurative use of language. The allusions to crucifixion in the turtle passage come with a number of implications—the painful nature of the turtles' deaths, their status as the innocent victims of the brutality of others, etc. We likewise want to identify an author's tone and consider its appropriateness and effectiveness given the rhetorical situation. As when crafting an argument, we should attend to these details when presented with an argument. If we understand that words both reveal and shape our sense of reality, we cannot help but give language the attention it deserves.

REFERENCES

Batchelor, H. (Winter 1994). Sex education: Have we gone too far? In *115 in the Shade: A Journal of English 115 Student Writing* (pp. 31–32). Provo, UT: BYU English Department.

Gold, H. (2002). *The age of happy problems.* New Brunswick, NJ: Transaction.

Gorgias. (2001). *Encomium of Helen* (M. Gagarin & P. Wood, Trans.). In V. B. Leitch (Ed.), *The Norton anthology of theory and criticism* (pp. 30–33). New York: Norton.

Hemingway, E. (1957). *A farewell to arms.* New York: Collier.

Kerferd, G. B. (1981). *The sophistic movement.* Cambridge, England: Cambridge University Press.

LeMann, N. (2000, October 16 & 23). The word lab: The mad science behind what the candidates say. *The New Yorker*, 100–112.

Murchison, B. (2002). Restrictions on school prayer are unfair to students. In W. Dudley (Ed.), *Religion in America: Opposing Viewpoints Series* (pp. 189–192). San Diego, CA: Greenhaven Press.

Nord, W. A. (2002). Public schools should include more religion in the curriculum. In W. Dudley (Ed.), *Religion in America: Opposing Viewpoints Series* (pp. 169–177). San Diego, CA: Greenhaven Press.

Swan, R. (2002). Parents must provide necessary medical treatment for children regardless of religious belief. In W. Dudley (Ed.), *Religion in America: Opposing Viewpoints Series* (pp. 142–149). San Diego, CA: Greenhaven Press.

NOTES

NOTES

NOTES

Chapter 7

FINDING THE AVAILABLE MEANS

Inventing an Argument

Kristine Hansen

INTRODUCTION

When most of us hear the word *invention,* we are likely to think first of such things as the airplane, the computer, the polio vaccine, or other devices and processes that smart people have developed through persistent study and experimentation. We usually think of inventors as creative geniuses who defy tradition and conventional wisdom as they work all alone in their laboratories to bring forth their brain children. While we rightly celebrate inventors like Thomas Edison or the Wright brothers, we often forget that they also built on the work of others; what they created grew out of their insights into existing principles and ideas and their ability to make connections between those principles and ideas. They made a new contribution, to be sure, but it was possible to do so because some things were already available to them. In this chapter you are going to learn about the process of rhetorical invention, that is, the process of creating arguments that will persuade others. You are going to learn that rhetorical invention does not depend solely on genius and isn't necessarily the result of solitary effort made in lonely study. While individual effort is certainly necessary, rhetorical invention is very much rooted in shared understandings, values, habits of mind, and ways of using language.

The inventors of rhetoric, the ancient Greeks, and the people who further refined rhetoric, the ancient Romans, understood invention as the process of producing reasons, ideas, examples, stories, facts, comparisons, analogies, and other verbal matter for an argument. They certainly would have thought of an argument as a new creation, but they would have regarded it as persuasive to the extent that it grew out of existing ideas and principles already accepted. The Latin roots of the word *invent* may help you see why they thought this way: *in* meant "on," and *venire* meant "to come." So to invent substance for rhetoric was to come upon it or find it. A new argument could be generated by visiting the places (*topoi* or "topics") that helped a speaker or a writer find a starting point for a new argument when it was called for by a given purpose, situation, and audience (rhetorical situation). So important is invention in rhetoric that Aristotle famously defined rhetoric as the art of finding the available means of persuasion in any case whatsoever. His book *Rhetoric* is a comprehensive treatise that systematically lays out all that was known about the art of communication in Greece of the fifth century, and three-fourths of the book deals with invention alone.

THE FIVE "CANONS" OF RHETORIC

Invention is the first of the five "canons," or categories, of rhetoric. In effect, invention amounts to planning what you will say; it's all the work you do before you begin writing a draft. The second canon of rhetoric, **arrangement**, concerns organizing the invented matter in a sequence that will be clear and persuasive to the audience. The third canon of rhetoric, **style**, deals with putting the invented material in the best words and word order (syntax); it includes deciding whether to use such flourishes as repetition, parallelism, rhythm, alliteration, irony, metaphor, and other figures of speech. Although we usually associate these stylistic devices only with literary writing, they are also important in other kinds of rhetoric. Often style is thought of as mere ornament, but, as Burton (2003) reminds us, the root of *ornament* suggests the importance and centrality of style, for Latin *ornare* means "to equip, fit out, or supply." In other words, to use style well means to suit your language to your invented matter so that it will have maximum impact on your audience and accomplish your intentions. The fourth and fifth canons, **memory** and **delivery**, remind us that rhetoric was originally the art of speaking well. Once a rhetor had invented and arranged ideas, then fitted them out in the best words and in the most effective syntax, the next task was to commit the invented speech to memory and then to deliver it to the audience effectively. Now that rhetoric has become a focus of study in writing courses, little attention is paid to memory; even in speech courses, students seldom learn the elaborate methods of memorizing speeches that were taught in the past. But delivery still has an important analog in writing, as a carelessly edited and sloppily printed paper does not impress a reader any more than a speaker who mumbles, fidgets, and looks at the floor impresses a listener. This chapter addresses invention, Chapter 8 deals with arrangement, and Chapter 9 attends to style and delivery.

Nowadays, the names of the five canons of rhetoric are not generally used in textbooks about writing. Instead of invention, such books speak of planning, prewriting, or pre-drafting. Textbooks usually use the word organization instead of arrangement; they might also speak of typical patterns for different genres of writing, such as instructions or letters. While the term style is still used, the scope of what is treated under that heading is usually much narrower than in past centuries, often being limited to a treatment of rules of grammar, usage, punctuation, and mechanics. Instead of oral delivery, you are now more likely to be taught about document design so that the format of your writing will aid the reader's ability to understand. Even though the names of the parts of rhetoric have changed, it is clear that certain principles of clear communication have persisted through the centuries.

TWO APPROACHES TO INVENTION

Likewise, it is probably true to say that a persistent challenge for students, whether they lived in ancient Greece or Rome, during the European Renaissance, or in the twenty-first century, is to come up with smart things to say to impress the teacher and other readers. Do you find as you write an academic paper that the most time-consuming and agonizing part of the process is generating enough strong material to support your main claim and persuade your audience to accept it? Corbett (1965) states that a writer "must either *have* something to say or *find* something to say" (p. 94, emphasis in original). Sometimes students your age feel that they neither have enough to say nor know where to find more. That's why teachers over the centuries have tried two approaches to helping students be inventive in their rhetoric.

The first approach is to try to store students' minds with ideas and information the students can draw from later by having the students read books, listen to lectures, observe nature, and seek other experiences that will add to the knowledge they can turn to when they need to create an argument. The great Roman teacher Quintilian, for example, stressed giving young people a broad education in history, music, math, astronomy, and literature, so that when they were grown citizens they would be able to draw on their education to create rhetoric that would make their cities and nations better. Quintilian and many other teachers in past centuries helped students create this fund of knowledge by assigning imitation exercises in school; for example, the students would write prose paraphrases of poetry they read or verse paraphrases of prose passages, or they would write papers in which they drew a moral from a fable, from biography, or from a historical event that they retold. Then they would often memorize and recite what they had written. By practicing the language arts in this manner, students developed a copious store of information and a facility with words that helped them generate things to say when they faced novel rhetorical situations. The general education requirements that you fulfill at college grow out of this teaching tradition by exposing students to great ideas and moments in the history of our civilization. Hopefully, all that you are learning in your science, literature, history, and arts courses is creating a storehouse of knowledge in your mind that you can turn to when you need to invent matter for an argument. For example, the lessons you learn in a physical science class may come in handy as you craft an argument on the effects of global warming, or your history class's discussion of the Founding Fathers and the drafting of the Constitution may influence an argument on church-state separation.

The second approach teachers have tried—and this approach complements the first, so they are not mutually exclusive—is teaching students how to find an argument by giving them strategies and locations from which material can be generated. Like Quintilian, Cicero believed in giving students a broad education to prepare them to be good citizen-rhetors; but both Cicero and Aristotle also devised methods of helping students find or generate new matter for an argument. They outlined strategies called the "topics" and the "stases" for thinking systematically about the issue at hand. Both of these strategies will be discussed in this chapter along with research in the library and on the Internet as ways of finding the available means of persuasion for papers you are assigned to write.

COMMON TOPICS OF INVENTION

While you have the Internet at your fingertips to stimulate your thinking and help you locate facts and ideas when you are assigned a paper, students in the past had the topics. Today we think of a topic as something you write *about,* but in the past a **topic** (from Greek *topos*) was thought of as a *place* to find an argument. This meaning of topic is still preserved in words like *topical ointment,* a salve that you apply to an affected place on your skin, or *topographical map,* a map that tries to show the actual features of a landscape by giving the elevations within the area it represents. Perhaps the most famous lists of topics for invention come from Aristotle, who taught that all discourse could be divided into three categories: forensic or judicial speeches, deliberative or legislative speeches, and epideictic or ceremonial speeches. For each of these types of speeches, Aristotle listed special topics the speaker could go to in order to invent appropriate and persuasive things to say if he had to persuade a jury of his innocence, for example, or encourage fellow legislators to vote for a new law, or deliver the eulogy at a funeral.

But Aristotle also listed a number of common topics to stimulate invention for any kind of discourse, for any occasion, speaker, or audience. These topics are ways of thinking about an issue and are meant to help generate premises for making rhetorical arguments. They are common not only because they are suited for any rhetorical situation but also because they represent shared habits of mind, values, and language use. Thus, they are effective starting points for building an argument because the audience is already disposed to accept the logic implicit in them. Students today can still use these topics as starting places for constructing arguments or as heuristics to guide their thinking. (The word *heuristic* comes from Greek *heuriskein*, meaning "to find.") Table 1 lists some of these common topics, using names and categories that various scholars have suggested from reading Aristotle and other theorists. Each topic is followed by an illustration of how it might be used to create an argument, either pro or con, about the issue of globalization. Note that you may not agree with some of these arguments, but that is beside the point. Each topic can be used to generate a number of arguments but doesn't guarantee their acceptance.

Table 1. *Names and Illustrations of Some Common Topics*

1.	Definition by class or category	Globalization is simply one more means of spreading democracy and freedom.
2.	Division of whole into parts	Globalization is a four-faceted phenomenon that affects nations economically, politically, culturally, and physically.
3.	Division into essence and accidents	Globalization is simply the spread of market economies throughout the world; everything else that changes in a country experiencing globalization is just a by-product.
4.	Comparison by similarity	Globalization, like nineteenth-century imperialism, extracts the wealth from less-developed nations, leaving them poorer, while enriching powerful nations and corporations that have advanced technologies and great economic capital.
5.	Comparison by difference	Unlike nineteenth-century imperialism, globalization increases the wealth of every nation affected by it through expanding competition and making markets more efficient.

6.	Comparison by degree	Globalization differs from nineteenth-century colonization only in the fact that multinational corporations don't take over the governments of the nations they enter.
7.	Cause and effect	Third World nations that lowered tariffs and deregulated international business have lowered their poverty rates by accepting globalization.
8.	Antecedent and consequence	One consequence of globalization is increased urbanization, which brings more pollution to the planet, whose atmosphere is already warming from greenhouse gases.
9.	Contraries	Globalization is concentrating the world's wealth in the hands of a comparative few, so it must be promoting the poverty of all the rest.
10.	Contradictions	Outsourcing jobs either benefits the economy or it does not.
11.	Authority	According to the United Nations Human Development Report, globalization is creating new threats to human security.
12.	Testimonial	A young woman working in a U.S.-owned Nike factory in Thailand described how the workers were locked in the factory and permitted only one restroom break during an 8-hour workday.
13.	Statistics	Prof. Sala-i-Martin used 7 indexes to measure poverty around the globe, and he found there were between 300 and 500 million fewer poor people in 1998 than in the 1970s.
14.	Maxims	"A rising tide lifts all boats," so if global competition improves the standard of living of some people, eventually it will improve the standard of living for all.
15.	Precedents	The 40-year-old U.S. trade embargo on Cuba has failed to keep American products out of Cuba; attempts to regulate free trade elsewhere are likewise doomed to failure.

Some students might consider it artificial and cumbersome to refer to the above list of topics when considering an issue because their minds seem naturally to resort to thinking of ways to argue an issue from a definition or from authority. Other students, however, may find it very helpful—especially when they are stuck—to refer to this list of topics and see whether they can come up with a way of dividing the issue or of comparing it to something else, so they can invent a stronger argument. As noted in Chapter 2, you must consider your audience above all else and use the GASCAP principles as you plan the kinds of arguments that are likely to persuade your readers to accept the claim you want to make about an issue. For example, if you were writing a term paper arguing that globalization is good for the economies of Third World nations, your audience might accept the maxim "A rising tide lifts all boats" as relevant to your argument and possibly even accurate. But they likely would not find it a sufficient or typical argument to make about this issue. More likely, your audience would expect to see arguments that are grounded in authority, cause and effect, and statistics. So the particular topic or strategy of using a maxim to support your claim could only be a minor part of your invention process for such a paper.

THE STASES

Although the strategy of using the stases for invention was developed early in the history of rhetoric by the Greek Hermagoras, the Roman Cicero is usually given the credit for developing this idea fully, particularly to teach invention for judicial arguments. *Stases* is the plural of the word *stasis*, a Greek word that means "standstill." Thus, a **stasis** is a place on which an argument may stand or the point from which it can proceed. Table 2 gives the names of the four stases and questions to be asked about each.

Table 2. The Stases and Their Meanings

Fact	What is the issue? Does the issue exist? Is it true? Where did it come from? How did it begin? What is the cause? Can it be changed?
Definition	If the issue exists, what should it be called? How should it be defined? What kind is it? What are its parts and how are they related? To what class of things does the issue belong?
Quality	How serious or important is the issue? Is it good or bad, right or wrong, honorable or dishonorable?
Procedure	What should be done about the issue? What jurisdiction should take responsibility for the issue? What actions in regard to the issue are possible or desirable?

Using the stases to invent matter for an argument about an issue requires you to know your audience and their position with regard to the issue. Let's say you want to write a letter to one of the U.S. senators from your state asking him or her to introduce legislation intended to halt and even reverse global warming, a phenomenon that you think requires immediate action. But it would likely be pointless to tell the senator what kind of legislation you think should be introduced (a procedure) until you are sure that you and the senator both agree on the fact, the definition, and the quality of global warming. You need to find out which stasis or standpoint offers common ground for both you and the senator to start from in order to have a fruitful argument about this issue. So first you might look at the senator's website to see if there is any sort of position statement there about global warming; you could also look for news articles that would give you some idea of the senator's position on the issue. You would need to do this first because you want to find out whether the senator even considers global warming to be a **fact**. If you were to find a newspaper article stating that the senator considers all of the outcry about global warming to be just so much "science fiction," you would have to start at the first stasis because your immediate task would be to find arguments that persuade the senator that global warming is a fact.

But now suppose you find that the senator does agree that global warming exists; however, it is not a serious problem, just a temporary phenomenon that the planet undergoes from time to time. In that case, you would find the starting point for your argument at the second stasis, **definition**, and you would have to find arguments to persuade the senator to change his or her definition to match your definition of global warming as a human-caused phenomenon that might be reversible if the right actions are taken. Now suppose that the senator believed that global warming is a fact that should be defined as potentially catastrophic but that there is still plenty of time to deal with it. In that case, the point from which you would proceed is the third stasis, **quality**, because you would want to argue that the issue requires immediate action. Now suppose the senator agreed with you on the standpoint of quality; then it would be appropriate to move to the fourth stasis, **procedure**, and outline your argument for how to resolve the problem.

As you can see, using the stases as an invention strategy requires you to do a lot of background research about your audience so that you don't end up wasting your time arguing for what the audience already accepts or talking right past your audience because you haven't established the point at which you disagree. Using the stases as a heuristic narrows the scope of what you need to invent because you only need to make an argument about the stasis at issue. Debates in the United States about complex issues such as abortion or the role of religion in the public square are often not very fruitful because the people involved in these debates have not identified those parts of the issue they agree on, so they talk about everything at once. If they would proceed through the stases first, they could then focus on trying to persuade each other more systematically about the points where they disagree. The chances of reaching a consensus or a compromise are enhanced if the questions that are most urgently at issue are identified at the outset.

RESEARCH AS INVENTION

"The topics and the stases are all very fine and good," you might be saying at this point, "but what I have to write next is a research paper." If this is indeed your concern, you have identified an important means of invention all your professors will expect you to be able to use at college: library and Internet research. Inventing an argument through research is completely compatible with knowledge of the topics and stases because you will need to identify the type of information you find through your research in the library or on the Internet (you could do this with the topics) and decide the best way to use it in the argument you are constructing (you could do this with the stases). But before proceeding, we need to consider what a research-based issues paper requires you to do and what those requirements imply for the way you conduct your research.

The first requirement is that your research paper be an argument, not merely a compilation of what various authorities have said about an issue. This kind of paper may be new for you, as high school research papers often turn out to be mainly an exercise in finding and citing sources, and the main goal for many students is just to make the paper long enough. But the requirement of a research-based argument means that you must take a stand on a debatable issue. Rather than take a firm stand at the outset and then merely look for material to support it, it is best to approach your research with a sense of openness and questioning. So at first you should read your library and Internet sources to determine what stand you feel persuaded to take by those who have already thought and written about the issue. Going into your research with an open mind will be an advantage because you will be more likely to consider all sides of the issue carefully and thus take a position that is responsive to the complexities and nuances of the issue. In other words, you will be inventing your position as you read as well as inventing the substance of your paper by taking notes about all sides of the issue for later use.

Taking a well-informed and thoughtful position on the issue you choose will be important in creating a credible ethos and thus disposing your audience to give your argument careful scrutiny. Paying attention to your audience and to your ethos are the second and third requirements of your research-based argument. Having your audience clearly in mind from the beginning will be an advantage as you begin the process of finding sources. You must not only choose sources that will be persuasive to your audience, but you must show that you have not overlooked sources that are not in accord with your position. Your audience expects you to have arrived at your position on the issue after a careful and informed process of study. And if your audience is not inclined to agree with your position at the outset, they will particularly want to know why you have found counter-arguments unpersuasive. If you are to have credibility with your audience and gain a hearing for your claim, you must show that the reasons and evidence you offer for your claim are superior to those that could be advanced against your claim. As you can see, inventing your argument from the research you find will not be the work of a few hours—or even one long night of frantic reading and writing. The invention process for a research-based issues paper will need to extend over several days, if not weeks.

At this point it is important to note that rhetorical invention is not a completely explicable and tidy process. Although there are many aids to invention, such as the topics and stases, as well as various questions, checklists, and techniques explained in handbooks about writing, the best thing you can do as you are researching material for a paper is simply to allow yourself time to mull over the things you are reading and learning. Often, at the least expected times and places, you will have an "aha! moment" when something that you couldn't quite figure out suddenly becomes clear, or you see the way to resolve a contradiction, or the perfect illustration of a point comes to you. You simply must begin early enough to research, plan, and draft your paper so that you give yourself the maximum opportunity for these serendipitous moments to arise. Rather than thinking of your research as a distasteful chore to be gotten out of the way as quickly and painlessly as possible, think of it as a quest to discover the best information you can about an issue that is crucial to you and your audience; then think of your writing as the shaping of a compelling argument that will win the assent of your readers and even change their minds if necessary.

A (HYPOTHETICAL) CASE STUDY

To illustrate what I have been saying about inventing a claim and then an argument from research, let's consider a hypothetical case. A student, Sam, has decided to write his issue paper on prayer in public schools. At the beginning he thinks he knows what stand he wants to take: As a religious person who benefits from daily personal prayers, he believes that it would be a good thing for everyone to realize this benefit; and since most people go to public schools, if they learned there how to pray, he thinks they would be better off—and so would the entire nation as a result. So he begins his invention process thinking that eventually he will claim that prayer should be a daily part of the routine in public schools. But he is not sure this is the position he wants to take, so he begins his research with a willingness to change his mind as he reads and studies the various arguments that have already been made for and against prayer in public schools. He also begins his research with his audience in mind: the other members of his class. Sam knows that some of them are not religious at all and probably seldom or never pray, while others belong to various faiths, including Christians, Jews, Muslims, and Buddhists. Sam realizes that to invent a well-reasoned argument for this audience, he will have to be very thorough and thoughtful in his research.

The librarians at Sam's college have created background study guides in several general areas of interest to help first-year students follow a careful research process and avoid jumping to ill-founded conclusions. Sam downloads one on "Church and State in America," which directs him to read specialized encyclopedias, other reference works, and key articles that have already been identified as good background reading for this broad issue. As he reads, he begins to see that the issue is very complex and it has a long history. Intrigued all the more, he continues reading until he gets a sense of the extent of the debate and of the terminology that has been used to discuss it, such words as *prayer, religion, public education, schools.* Eventually, because his teacher requires it, Sam formulates two questions he will try to answer in his research: "Why have the courts ruled against requiring prayer in public school? Do these court rulings infringe on the free exercise of religion?" Now he is ready to locate sources that will give him material for answers to these questions.

Using the various terms he found in his background reading, Sam searches for books that deal with this issue. His first search of his library's catalog using the search terms "religion" and "public schools" returns 232 titles—too many! Narrowing his search to "prayer" and "public schools," Sam gets 52 titles— still too many to read. He decides to look at those books that have been published since 1990, on the assumption that they will sum up the history of the issue prior to that time and reflect the latest thinking on the issue. That still leaves 22 books, so Sam eliminates duplicates, a specialized book for attorneys, and one with very specific local reference. He now has 16 book titles, but he notes that three of them are currently checked out and won't be back in time to use before his paper is due. Going to the library, he finds the remaining 13 books. At this point, Sam reminds himself of the questions he is trying to answer: "Why have the courts ruled against requiring prayer in public school? Do these court rulings infringe on the free exercise of religion?" By looking at the table of contents and the index of each book, he is able to identify seven books that discuss court rulings on the issue and explain the judicial thinking behind the rulings. He notes that two of the books have an obvious bias, as one author states in the preface that she is an atheist, and another states in his preface that he is president of a group that is lobbying Congress to amend the Constitution to allow prayer in schools. But Sam figures it will be interesting to read what they have to say, so he checks these books out along with the others. As you can see, even though Sam has had to go through a rather lengthy process to get to the point where he can start reading about his issue in depth, it really only took about four hours. Sam's investment of time will pay off later, as he is not just grabbing any sources he can find, but selecting from all the ones available those that will help him invent an argument from the best current thinking about the issue.

Next Sam searches databases for periodical articles on the issue, using the search terms he identified. Once again, a daunting number of possible articles show up on the screen, but through a process of narrowing the search terms and winnowing out titles that are old, extreme, or not helpful, Sam comes up with a manageable number of articles. For some of these he can download the full text online; however, some he must look up in the periodicals of the college library. Before spending money on photocopies, Sam skims the articles, especially the abstract when available, to see if the article is one he wants to read thoroughly.

Armed with his books and articles, Sam now heads home. But that evening at home, he also decides to see what he can find on the Internet. Both his teacher and the librarians who created the background study guide have warned Sam that much information on the Internet is not reliable, so Sam turns first to Internet search engines recommended by his college library: INFOMINE, Internet Public Library, Librarians' Index to the Internet, Libraryspot, Refdesk.com, and Search Engine Showdown. He learned that these search engines will lead him to websites, electronic journals, and online documents that have been peer reviewed and deemed credible. At the end of his first day of research, Sam now has 7 books, 10 articles, and 5 web texts to work from—more than his teacher requires, but he can still eliminate those that are not helpful, redundant, or skewed. The available means of inventing his argument are now at hand.

Sam spends his research time the next few days reading and taking notes on his laptop computer. Soon he begins to see categories that he can sort his notes into, so he creates files for each category and saves his notes in the appropriate files. He is careful to put quotation marks around any words and sentences he copies directly from the source, along with page numbers and authors. Whenever he summarizes or paraphrases a source, he also writes the page numbers and authors. He knows he will have to document every borrowed idea in his paper, and he knows that nothing will undermine his credibility more than plagiarism. Sam wants his audience to be persuaded by his eventual argument, and he knows that part of the persuasion will come from how thorough and honest they perceive him to be.

As he continues to read and take notes, Sam finds his original position on school prayer shifting. Where he once favored making prayer a required part of the school day, he now begins to understand and accept the reasoning behind the court rulings that disallow required prayer. He learns that the First

Amendment to the Constitution has consistently been interpreted to mean that the government cannot establish a preferred religion for the citizens of the country. Because public schools are run by the government, if they were to require students to participate in prayer, that would be like establishing a preferred religion, as it would be impossible to have a nondenominational prayer that satisfied the adherents of all possible religions—Christian, Jewish, Islamic, Buddhist, and so on—as well as those who do not adhere to any religion. Even allowing some students not to participate in the prayer wouldn't solve the dilemma because that would, in its way, still establish a religion by favoring believers over non-believers. To help make this point, Sam decides that he will quote from the U.S. Supreme Court ruling in *Santa Fe v. Doe* (2000): "School sponsorship of a religious message is impermissible because it sends the ancillary message to members of the audience who are non-adherents that they are outsiders, not full members of the political community, and an accompanying message to adherents that they are insiders, favored members of the political community." Sam has now found a position with respect to the first question he set out to answer: "Why have the courts ruled against requiring prayer in public school?"

But he still needs to answer his second question: "Do these court rulings infringe on the free exercise of religion?" At first it seemed to Sam that the answer was yes, because by not allowing prayer in school for those who would like to have it, the courts seem to prefer the interests of non-believers over those of believers. That in itself seems to be a way that the state "establishes" religion, i.e., by declaring it unimportant. But as Sam reads his sources, he learns that the courts have not ruled out *any* prayer in public school, but only *required* prayers led by teachers, who are employees of the government. Again and again, Sam reads that in the various court rulings, the judges have made clear that students can form groups that pray together at the school or study the Bible or any other religious book. It seems that students are able to freely exercise their religious beliefs while at school, but the school employees cannot require students to participate in religious observances. Sam decides that to help make this point he will quote from a 1998 directive from the U.S. Department of Education, which states the following:

Schools may not forbid students acting on their own from expressing their personal religious views or beliefs solely because they are of a religious nature. Schools may not discriminate against private religious expression by students, but must instead give students the same right to engage in religious activity and discussion as they have to engage in other comparable activity. Generally, this means that students may pray in a nondisruptive manner during the school day when they are not engaged in school activities and instruction, subject to the same rules of order that apply to other student speech. (Riley, 1998)

So after about 12 hours of reading and note-taking, Sam is now prepared to craft a claim about this issue that he will use as the thesis of his argument: "The courts have ruled correctly that public schools may not require students to participate in prayers as part of the curriculum because such a requirement would amount to violating the constitutional ban on a state-established religion. However, the courts have also ruled correctly that students may voluntarily participate in extracurricular prayer on school premises because to forbid them from doing so would violate their constitutional right to the free exercise of religion. In both cases, the court has made clear that the position of the school with respect to religion must be one of neutrality." Sam realizes that he may change this statement of his thesis as he drafts and revises his paper, but for now he has a claim that is more informed and more nuanced than his original position. And it is one that he can defend well in his paper for the audience that will read his paper. Even though he is a religious person who values prayer, Sam doesn't feel that he is being untrue to his principles by taking this stand. From his research, he has come to realize that he lives in a society with all kinds of religions and all degrees of adherence to the teachings of those religions. Thus, he has come to view the court rulings as the best possible solution to an issue that could be terribly divisive in a pluralist society. Sam feels confident that he can now explain this position to an audience and support it with the best available evidence.

CONCLUSION:
JOINING THE CONVERSATION

Sam's story illustrates how doing research is both a process of finding the available material to support your position *and* a process of establishing the position you will take. There is an interplay between these two processes that you should welcome as you immerse yourself in finding and reading the best sources you can locate. In these sources you will find reasons, analogies, facts, statistics, authorities, testimonials, precedents, anecdotes, causes, effects, and a number of other means of persuasion that you can use in your argument—in short, you will find material that can be classified using the common topics of invention and applied to whatever stasis is relevant for the audience you are addressing. By finding these materials and weaving them together to make your own argument, you enter the grand conversation about the important issues that face us, a conversation that sustains both scholarly and civic life. This conversation was described in the following way by a twentieth-century rhetorician named Kenneth Burke:

> Imagine that you enter a parlor. You come late. When you arrive, others have long preceded you, and they are engaged in a heated discussion, a discussion too heated for them to pause and tell you exactly what it is about. In fact, the discussion had already begun long before any of them got there, so that no one present is qualified to retrace for you all the steps that had gone before. You listen for a while, until you decide that you have caught the tenor of the argument; then you put in your oar. (pp. 110–111)

Strong rhetorical invention gives you the means to "put in your oar"—to take a turn in the conversation even though you are only a young college student and others older and wiser than you seem to have already said everything that could be said. Even though a lot has already been said, no one will have made the argument quite like you can. The continuation of society depends on this conversation continuing, so you must take your turn, even though you may think you are too young and inexperienced to do so. As you grow older, it will be even more important for you to participate in this conversation as a citizen of this nation and of the world, and it will be critical for you to help teach the next generation how a democracy sustains itself through argument. The course you are now taking in writing and argumentation is not just a hoop you jump through so you can get a diploma; it will be the foundation of your college education and your preparation for civic life. You have an academic and a civic responsibility to know what others have said about the issues that face us, to use the available means of invention to define and establish your own positions, and to make them as persuasive as possible so that you can influence the course of the society you live in.

REFERENCES

Burke, K. (1941). *The philosophy of literary form.* Berkeley: University of California Press.

Burton, G. (2003). Style. *Silva rhetoricae: The forest of rhetoric.* Retrieved May 25, 2006, from http://humanities.byu.edu/rhetoric/silva.htm

Corbett, E. (1965). *Classical rhetoric for the modern student.* New York: Oxford University Press.

Riley, R. (1998). *Secretary's statement on religious expression.* Retrieved May 25, 2006, from http://www.ed.gov/Speeches/08-1995/religion.html

Santa Fe Independent School District v. Doe, 530 U.S. 290, 390 (2000).

NOTES

NOTES

NOTES

Chapter 8

ARRANGING AN ARGUMENT

Form and Function

Grant M. Boswell

INTRODUCTION

By now you know something about arguments and invention in the rhetorical tradition of argumentation. Following invention, the second canon of the rhetorical tradition is arrangement or judgment. A canon in its original sense is a standard for measuring, but we use the term now in the sense of a rule or guiding principle. Both arrangement and judgment treat the ways to lay out an argument for the reader, but the guiding principle is form.

What do we mean by **form**? This is a difficult question, but I would like to approach it in terms of how readers respond to what they read. Let me start with a question that I hope will allow us to get at a working definition of form. Try to remember when you were young and one of your parents or a sibling or a teacher read a book to you. If you were like many small children, you liked to hear the same story over and over again. In fact, you probably had your favorite bedtime story memorized. If your mother or father read it to you and slipped up, you would correct them, or if you were really obsessive, you might make them start over. Why did you do that? Why do children like to hear the same story over and over again and insist that the reader get it right?

Now think of a book or a movie or a song that you like. How many times have you read it, seen it, heard it? Why do you keep reading, watching, listening to it? Nothing really changes. The hero in the book or movie doesn't get killed the thirteenth time through; the unrequited love of the forlorn vocalist isn't magically rewarded if you keep replaying the song. Why do we keep reading the same books, watching the same movies, listening to the same songs when the outcome doesn't change? Because we get a great deal of satisfaction in seeing things unfold as we have come to expect. That is the power and the pleasure of form.

As writers we might learn something by considering the power of form. Form keeps readers reading to make sure their formal expectations are met. To employ a powerful tool such as form, however, places some heavy obligations on us as writers. We wouldn't want to violate our readers' sense of form by not meeting their expectations. That might have disastrous consequences for us as writers.

READERS READING

To understand what those disastrous consequences might be, let's consider your habits as a reader. What do you read when you don't have to read for school? Newspapers? News magazines? Trade magazines? Novels? Biographies? Science fiction? Let's say that you are reading the paper. How do you read it? Do you start with the headlines? The comics? The sports page? The society page? Business? My grandmother used to go straight to the obituaries because she wanted to see if anyone she knew had died recently. We all read what we find interesting, entertaining, enjoyable, or relevant. Suppose you are in the market for a used car. On a normal day you might pick up the paper and go straight for the crossword puzzle, but today you go to the classified ads to look for a deal on a car. That is, a particular interest can take priority over something you usually enjoy. We all read what we find enjoyable, but sometimes what is interesting and relevant can take precedence.

Now ask yourself what you do when you read an article in a magazine or in a newspaper and you get to the bottom of the page and find that the article is continued on page 139 or in section B. Do you take the trouble to find the rest of the article and read it? You do only if you are really interested in it. Most of the time you probably say, "Oh well, it isn't that interesting," and you move on to another article or section of the paper. This is the way we generally read. We read what we are interested in, and when it ceases to be interesting or is too much trouble, we stop and go on to something else.

As writers we need to remember that our readers are just like we are: they won't keep reading unless they are kept reading by something they find interesting, enjoyable, or relevant. As writers we need to remember that real readers, unlike teachers, don't have to read to the end. It would be disastrous for us as writers to write an argument and have our reader stop reading midway through the second page. We would have lost the opportunity to present our case in its entirety; we would have lost the opportunity to influence our reader. But as writers we now know that form is a very useful and powerful tool to keep readers reading. Clearly, we need to know more about form and how it works.

DEFINING FORM

I like Kenneth Burke's definition of form. Burke was one of the great rhetoricians of the twentieth century and his definition of form is right on: "Form in literature is an arousing and fulfilling of desires. A work has form in so far as one part of it leads a reader to anticipate another part, to be gratified by the sequence" (1968, p. 124). Although Burke is talking about form in literature, form works the same way in nearly everything else you can think of. Think of every sit-com you've ever seen. Some situation is disrupted by an event and, as a viewer, you feel compelled to see how the situation is resolved. This is the basic pattern: scene, disturbance, resolution. It is also the basic form of most novels, stories, jokes, movies, and songs. Some kind of expectation is created and you feel compelled to see the expectation fulfilled.

When the fulfillment is unsatisfactory, you feel cheated. Have you ever seen a movie that ends in a way you didn't expect or in which the plot isn't fully resolved? Sometimes such endings can be a pleasant surprise, but other times you leave the theater disappointed. What you were longing for was for your expectations to be fulfilled and they weren't. It is a very unsatisfying feeling. But that is the power of form. We want to see our desires fulfilled; we want our expectations met; we want to see problems solved; we want to have doubts resolved; we want our questions answered. And we will stick around until they are fulfilled, met, solved, resolved, or answered.

There is a good story about the power of form I like to tell my students. I heard it once and don't know if it is true, but it is a good story. The child prodigy Mozart was like most other children in that he didn't like to get up in the mornings. His mother learned that if she played a chord sequence and left it unresolved, Mozart would have to get up and resolve it. But then he was up. I hope it is true because it illustrates the power of form so well.

So now we know that form has strong appeal for us. It kept us listening to our bedtime stories to make sure they were read to us just as we had come to expect. It keeps us watching the same movies, listening to the same songs, reading the same books for the very same reason. It keeps us watching, listening to, or reading something to see how our expectations will be fulfilled even when we may not be all that interested. So how does this knowledge help us as writers?

THE PARAGRAPH AND FORM

Let's talk about form at the paragraph level first. Once we have learned how form works in paragraphs, we can extrapolate and apply the same principle to an entire paper. You probably know that every paragraph needs to have a point. On reading comprehension tests you may have been taught to look for the sentence that states the point of the paragraph. Sometimes this is called the topic sentence. As writers you probably have been taught to include topic sentences in your paragraphs. It turns out that this is very good advice. Why? Because readers expect paragraphs to have points.

We just learned that whenever readers, viewers, or listeners have expectations, those expectations need to be met, or the readers, viewers, and listeners will feel cheated. And now we know why they feel cheated: their formal expectations have not been met. So paragraphs must have points or readers feel cheated. This is very useful information for writers. The last thing you as a writer want to do is make your reader feel cheated. So where does the point of a paragraph have to occur? Where do readers expect the point of the paragraph to be? We need to know the answer to this question so we can meet our readers' expectations for form at the paragraph level. Readers expect the point of the paragraph to be in one of two places: at the beginning or at the end. Either place will do, but putting the point in the middle of the paragraph will not do because that is not where readers expect it. Let's take the most common case in paragraphs: the point-first paragraph.

POINT-FIRST PARAGRAPHS

Most of the paragraphs you read are **point-first paragraphs**. The point of the paragraph, the sentence that sums everything up or that states the main idea in its most general form, usually comes at the beginning of the paragraph. The rest of the sentences in the paragraph amplify, qualify, illustrate, or specify the point, adding information, comparing or contrasting, or increasing the level of specificity. That is the way most paragraphs work in English.

Take, for example, the paragraph you just read. The point of the paragraph is the first sentence: "Most of the paragraphs you read are point-first paragraphs." The second sentence amplifies this point by repetition. The third sentence adds additional information. The fourth sentence adds information about how paragraphs function and provides closure. That's it. That is how most paragraphs in English work. The formal expectation is created by stating the point in the first or second sentence (in a long paragraph possibly even the third sentence) and adding information to the point. As long as the point occurs early in the paragraph and as long as the rest of the sentences are relevant to the point, the readers' expectations are fulfilled and the paragraph is well formed. In point-first paragraphs the point serves two functions: it creates the expectation for what is to follow, and it states the point.

POINT-LAST PARAGRAPHS

I mentioned, however, that not all paragraphs are point-first paragraphs. And since we know that the point can't occur in the middle because readers don't expect it there, the only other option is for the point to occur at the end. These paragraphs are called **point-last paragraphs**, and although they are not as common as point-first paragraphs, they can teach us something very important about form.

Let's take a look at the paragraph you just read. What's the point? I think the point is the last sentence: "These paragraphs are called **point-last paragraphs**, and although they are not as common as point-first paragraphs, they can teach us something very important about form." But if it's a point-last paragraph how is it well formed? In the point-first paragraph we noticed that the point served two functions: first to create an expectation, second to state the point. In a point-last paragraph the point is obviously stated at the end, so what creates the expectation? In the paragraph above the first sentence does: "I mentioned, however, that not all paragraphs are point-first paragraphs." The first sentence signals that there is an exception to what we learned earlier. The "however" tells you that a contrast is coming, so you expect one. That expectation is met when you learn that point-last paragraphs can teach us something very important about form.

So, what do point-last paragraphs teach us about form? We know that form is the creation and fulfillment of an expectation. And we know that in a point-last paragraph the point—that is, the fulfillment—is at the end. So there has to be something at the beginning to create the expectation. Point-first paragraphs do the same thing, only the topic sentence has to do double duty: it has to both create the expectation and state the point. A point-last paragraph, however, teaches us that the creation of an expectation and its fulfillment can be separated for effect, and this two-fold sense of form is the one that many arguments employ, and there is a good reason for this.

MANAGING INFORMATION

The point-last model of form at the paragraph level will be important later, so I want you to remember it, but right now we need to learn something else about form at the paragraph level that will also be useful when we talk about the form of an entire argument. We know that paragraphs have to have a point, but there is something else that paragraphs have to do to be formally complete: paragraphs have to manage information according to reader expectations. So we need to know what we mean by "information" and what reader expectations are for managing information at the paragraph level.

Information comes in two flavors: old and new. **Old information** is information you can assume that your readers already know from general knowledge or information that you have already mentioned. Once you mention a bit of information it becomes old information. **New information** is information that you can't assume your readers already know or information that you haven't already mentioned. That's easy enough, but what expectation do readers have for how old and new information is managed?

It so happens that English-speaking readers have very definite expectations of how they want their information managed. Readers expect old information to be placed at the beginning of sentences and new information after the main verb. So a good sentence should manage information by placing information that your readers already know or that you have already mentioned at the beginning of the sentence, usually in the subject. New information, the stuff your readers may not know or that you haven't mentioned yet, goes after the verb or in the predicate. So the information flow of English sentences is old to new. Let's take a look at the sentence you just read. The subject is "information flow." I have already mentioned information and its management, so "information flow" can reasonably be assumed to be old information. The verb is "is," and the predicate is the verb plus the rest of the sentence. So the new information is "is old to new." This description of the relation of old and new information is something I have not mentioned before, so it is new information and is appropriately placed in the predicate.

But this is management of information at the sentence level. What do readers expect of information managed at the paragraph level? Readers expect that the old information in a paragraph will be fairly consistent. That is, if you underline all the subjects in the main clauses of the sentences in a paragraph, you should see that there is some consistency in the underlined words. Let's look at a paragraph I wrote earlier to see how I did at managing old and new information. I am going to underline the subjects of the main clauses to see if they form a relatively consistent string of old information.

> <u>I</u> like Kenneth Burke's definition of form. <u>Burke</u> was one of the great rhetoricians of the twentieth century and <u>his definition of form</u> is right on: "Form in literature is an arousing and fulfilling of desires. A work has form in so far as one part of it leads a reader to anticipate another part, to be gratified by the sequence" (1968, p. 124). Although Burke is talking about form in literature, <u>form</u> works the same way in nearly everything else you can think of. Think of every sit-com you've ever seen. <u>Some situation</u> is disrupted by an event and, as a viewer, you feel compelled to see how the situation is resolved. <u>This</u> is the basic pattern: scene, disturbance, resolution. <u>It</u> is also the basic form of most novels, stories, jokes, movies, and songs. <u>Some kind of expectation</u> is created and you feel compelled to see the expectation fulfilled.

I am going to list the words I have underlined and then describe whether the word is old information.

I	"I" (writer) known (old info)
Burke	mentioned in previous sentence (old info)
his definition of form	already mentioned (old info)
form	mentioned (old info)
Some situation	not mentioned (new info—oops!)
This	refers to preceding concept (old, but vague)

| It | refers to pattern mentioned (old info) |
| Some kind of expectation | mentioned previously (old info) |

This is a very helpful exercise for two reasons. First, it tells me if I have managed old and new information according to reader expectations. If we look at the list of words, we can see a string of old information that centers around "Burke's definition of form." So I didn't do too badly. When we manage old information consistently in paragraphs, we produce what is called **cohesion**. This paragraph is fairly cohesive because the old information is managed fairly consistently. The consistency of old information gives the reader the sense that we are on topic. But the second reason this process is useful is that I can make the paragraph more cohesive by revising. I can revise the sentence beginning with "Some situation..." by adding a phrase: "In sit-coms some situation..." This addition ties the sentence a little better to the previous quote from Burke that discusses form in literature. And I can revise the sentence beginning with "This" to read "This sequence," referring to the sequence already mentioned of situation, disturbance, and resolution. This revision would make the old information more explicit and, therefore, improves the cohesion. I recommend checking for cohesion as a revision strategy. If you ever get a comment in the margin such as "I can't make sense of this paragraph" or "I'm having a hard time following you here," chances are the paragraph is incohesive because you have not managed information according to reader expectations.

To sum up, for a paragraph to be well formed it has to have a point. The point usually occurs at the beginning, but it can also occur at the end. If the point occurs at the end, the paragraph has to have a sentence at the beginning that creates an expectation in the reader as to what the point might be. And finally, the paragraph has to manage information on the sentence level from old to new and produce cohesive strings of old information among the sentences.

FORM AND THE ARGUMENT

Now that we know how form works at the paragraph level, we can make the jump to hyperspace and see how the same principle of form works at the discourse level, or at the level of the paper. We have two models for form. Let's talk about the merits of each. The first is when the opening statement has to perform the two functions of creating the expectation and stating the point. If we use this model, we are talking about something you are already familiar with. It is the use of the thesis statement at the beginning of your paper. The thesis statement usually tells your reader what the point of your essay will be. Moreover, the thesis statement does create an expectation, although a minimal one. The only real expectation that a traditional thesis statement creates in your reader is whether you provide the evidence to support the point that you have already announced. This is not much of an expectation, but there are some genres of writing in which this is the preferred way of establishing the formal parameters of your paper.

Many proposals are written in this way. Whoever is going to evaluate the proposal wants to know up front what the proposal is in order to evaluate the rest of the evidence in light of the proposal. Much academic writing falls into this same mode of reading. The teacher wants to know up front what your point is in order to evaluate the rest of the essay in light of the point you have already announced. The teacher then grades you on how well you did what you said you were going to do. A thesis statement that both announces the point of the essay and creates an expectation, albeit a minimal expectation, is often found in writing that has to be evaluated for approval or for a grade. And since most of the writing you are doing at the university is academic writing, you would be well advised to follow the traditional thesis-first model. You may want to discuss this with your writing teacher to see if he or she has a preference. The important points for you to remember are these. First, you must create some expectation in order to set the formal expectations for your paper. Second, you must meet your readers' expectations. If your teacher expects a thesis-first approach, then by all means meet that expectation. To do otherwise might jeopardize your grade.

For some rhetorical situations, however, the traditional thesis statement at the beginning of the essay that announces the point of your essay is not always a good idea. Why not? Remember that we defined the claim in Chapter 2 as initially unacceptable to your reader. What do you think would happen if you announced to a real reader a thesis or a claim that was initially unacceptable? Readers don't read anything they don't find interesting or relevant. If you were to announce a thesis that your reader finds unacceptable, the reader is likely to do one of two things. The reader might simply dismiss the paper because of the unacceptable claim and move on to that re-run on TV, or the reader might go ahead and read the argument, but do so with a resistant attitude. Either way your chances of making an argument that actually influences the reader are diminished. So, what I am telling you is that the traditional thesis statement, although useful for some genres of writing, is not always the best choice in an argumentative essay. So if you don't put a thesis statement that announces your point at the beginning of the essay, what do you do?

The principle of the thesis statement is sound in that an expectation has to be made to create a sense of form for your reader. The announcement of an initially unacceptable point, however, will probably work against you in an argument. But remember what we learned from the point-last paragraph? You can make your point, that is, arrive at your claim at the end of your essay, but you still have to create an expectation for your reader at the beginning without tipping your hand. We mentioned earlier that form is created by creating an expectation, by posing a problem, by making a promise, or by asking a question. These are all good strategies for setting the formal constraints of your paper for two reasons: first, they have the advantage of creating a much stronger expectation for your reader than merely announcing what you plan to do. Asking a good question can keep the reader reading. Second, a good question has the advantage of not telling your reader what your claim is, a claim the reader is likely to object to right off the bat. So the model of form from the point-last paragraph is a much better model for setting the formal constraints of an argument when addressing a potentially hostile audience because it creates a genuine expectation in your reader and it does not put your reader off.

So now we know that a question is a good way to create an expectation and set the formal parameters of an argument. Where are we going to find a good question? Arguments arise from **questions at issue**. If you have done your argumentative analysis and know what is at issue for your reader, then you already have a good question. You can, in fact, use your issue question to create an expectation for your reader. Typically, the question would be posed to your reader at the end of your introduction. In creating a strong expectation for our reader by posing the question at issue, you are setting the formal constraints of your paper by the parameters set forth in the issue question. I say constraints because you are constraining the reader and you are constraining yourself to those parameters.

THE READER/WRITER CONTRACT

We call the use of the issue question, or some other means, to create a strong expectation in your reader the **reader/writer contract**. Like all contracts, the reader/writer contract binds both parties. The reader promises implicitly to keep reading so long as the writer addresses the question at issue. If the writer ever strays and becomes irrelevant, gets off topic, or writes in a way the reader doesn't perceive as addressing the question, the reader is justified in stopping reading. I know this may sound harsh, but one of the most useful comments a teacher can make on a student paper is this: "If I didn't have to read this paper, I would stop right here because I can't see how this paragraph relates to the question you posed in your introduction."

The reader/writer contract obligates both reader and writer— the reader to keep reading, the writer to be relevant to the question at issue. If the reader ceases reading, he or she can be accused of not giving the argument a fair shot and of being closed-minded. If the writer gets off topic, he or she has broken the contract and the reader can justifiably stop reading and move on to something else. A broken contract is a serious problem for the writer of an argument because he or she gives up the opportunity to present the best case and loses the opportunity to address the reader on an issue of mutual importance.

A writer then must set the formal constraints of the argument by making a reader/writer contract. The contract can be made by using the issue question, but it must be something that keeps the reader reading and does not put the reader off by announcing the point or the claim of the argument. In this way form at the essay level works very similarly to form at the paragraph level. But the similarity between the essay and the paragraph does not stop at creating an expectation to keep the reader reading and to keep the writer on topic.

MANAGING OLD AND NEW CONCEPTS

In fact, we can manage information at the essay level according to the same principle that we learned by making paragraphs cohesive. We can discuss old information first and move from old to new information. To avoid confusion, we probably should not talk about "information" at the level of the essay because we are really dealing with concepts in an argument rather than bits of information in a paragraph. But the principle is sound. We can begin our argument with an "old" concept, a concept familiar to our reader. How do we know what is familiar to our reader?

We can return to our issue question. A question at issue generates the conditions for arguments. We can reasonably assume that if we have analyzed the situation carefully and have discovered the question that seems to be at issue for those who are making arguments, then we know what the issue question is. But more than that, we also know that the issue question poses a potential relationship between concepts. Let's examine an issue question to see how this might work:

> What consequence does making illegal immigration a felony have on the security of our borders?

This question asserts a relation between two concepts: making illegal immigration a felony [concept A] and the security of our borders [concept B]. Since both concepts make up the question at issue and the issue is important to our reader, we can assume that both concepts are familiar to our reader. So in beginning an argument you would want to write an introduction. A good historical narrative that gives the history of the problem and frames the current issue would work well. Or you could try a "some say this, some say that" introduction in which you summarize the position of those who favor making illegal immigration a felony and those who do not. Or there are several other possible ways of writing an introduction. Once you have written your introduction, you then make a reader/writer contract. We can use our issue question as our contract.

Now we are ready to launch our argument. Let's begin with concept B, the security of our borders. We can talk about all kinds of things with respect to our borders: their length; the remoteness of long stretches of the borders; the difficulty of patrolling long, remote borders; the agencies charged with the responsibility of patrolling the borders; the number of border-patrol workers; technology now employed to patrol the borders; technology being planned or developed for patrolling the borders; citizen-volunteer efforts to patrol the borders; security risks, both real and imagined, of a porous border. As you can see, we have a lot to talk about in discussing concept B.

Or we could start with concept A. We could discuss the proposal to make illegal immigration a felony. Who proposed it? Where? What is the current penalty for illegal immigration? How many illegal immigrants now reside in this country? How many are estimated to enter each year? What measures have been taken in the past? Did they work? We have just as much to talk about with concept A as we did with concept B, and either discussion would be a reasonable place to start because both concepts would be familiar to our reader (old information).

How we go about structuring the rest of the argument will require that we return to the entire argument that we developed in Chapter 2. The argument, as you may recall, consists of a claim that answers the issue question, a reason, and an assumption. In developing the entire argument, you must know what the parts of the argument are in order to lay them out in a reasonable sequence for your reader. Here's one version of the argument:

> Making illegal immigration a felony *decreases* the security of our borders because, as long as the US economy creates the "pull effect," the potential deterrence of the felony charge <u>will encourage</u> illegal immigrants to develop more sophisticated and daring means to enter our country.

We have already decided that after an introduction in which we make a reader/writer contract, we need to start with a concept already familiar to our reader. Since the claim consists of two concepts from our issue question, we can begin with either of them because both should be familiar to our reader. If you have done the conceptual work well in asking a good issue question, answering it with specific attention to your audience, providing a good reason, and checking your assumption to insure that it is acceptable to your intended audience, then you should be able to proceed through your argument in a way that makes sense to you and to your reader.

DISPOSING THE ARGUMENT

There are, however, a few guidelines that you will want to follow in laying out your argument. The technical term for laying out the argument is **disposition**. So, here are the guidelines for disposing the argument. Start with a concept familiar to your audience. Then move to another concept. You must discuss concepts before you relate them. Save the relationship between concepts for last because it is your claim and therefore your conclusion.

Just to make sure we all know what I am talking about, let's review all the parts and relations of the argument on illegal immigration. I will then lay out one possible disposition of the argument. Remember that in the claim we have concept A ("making illegal immigration a felony") and concept B ("the security of our borders"). They are related in the claim by the verb "decreases." Our reason with its parts labeled looks like this: "because, as long as the US economy creates the 'pull effect' [qualifier], the potential deterrence of the felony charge [repetition of concept A] *will encourage* illegal immigrants to develop more sophisticated and daring means to enter our country [concept C]." It is essential that the first concept of the reason be a repetition of concept A in the claim. The repetition of concept A in the reason provides the "lynch pin" that holds the argument together, since the question at issue centers on the consequences of making illegal immigration a felony. (Just to keep track of concept A, I have distinguished it in the reason by labeling it as A prime [A'].) Along with the reason, we can't forget the procatalepsis, or the anticipation of the reader's "buts." Last of all we know from Chapter 2 that there is an assumption that underlies the claim and reason. Below I will dispose the argument in an outline, estimating how many paragraphs I might write on each part and relation.

Introduction plus contract	Historical narrative	2 ¶'s
Concept B	Security of borders	2 ¶'s
Concept A	Proposal to felonize	1 ¶
Concept A'	Intent to deter by felonizing	1 ¶
Concept C	Sophisticated, daring means	2 ¶'s
Qualifier	The "pull effect"	1 ¶
A' will encourage C	Reason(s) meeting GASCAP criteria	2 ¶'s
Procatalepsis	Raise and meet objections	1 ¶
Whatever will encourage C also decreases B	Assumption as common ground	1 ¶
Therefore A decreases B	Conclusion	1 ¶
Disposition	Argument	14 ¶'s

I have tried to be conservative in estimating the number of paragraphs it would take to discuss the concepts and relations. As we saw above, there is a lot to say about each concept and, if you have done some research, a lot to say about your reason and procatalepsis. If you write about three paragraphs per page, the disposition schematized above is a four-page paper. If you expand the discussion of the concepts and relations, it can be much longer. The nice thing about disposing an argument as we have is that you can expand or contract it as needed. The basic argument can easily be done in three to four pages with a relatively basic discussion of concepts and relations. With some research and preparation, you can expand the argument into a much longer paper.

I want to emphasize that the scheme I outlined above is just one possible disposition of the argument. We could have just as easily started with Concept A, moved to A', then to C, then to the reason and procatalepsis, then to Concept B, then to the assumption, and finally to the conclusion. All you need to do is follow the guidelines for disposing an argument, and they are fairly simple: begin with an introduction and contract; start the argument with either Concept A or Concept B; discuss the other concepts of the argument before you relate them; save the relationship between Concept A and Concept B for last because it is your conclusion.

DISPOSITION AND PERSUASION

Now we know how to dispose an argument, but we may want to know how the disposition of an argument contributes to the overall persuasive force of the argument. We already learned that readers expect an essay to be well formed and that form has a very compelling effect on readers to keep reading. If we set up the argument with a reader/writer contract and make sure our argument sticks to the expectation we have created, then we will have met our readers' formal expectations. Moreover, in meeting our readers' expectations for form, we will also be assuring our readers that we have their best interest at heart. After all, we are meeting their formal expectations.

Readers also have expectations for reasonableness (logos). That is, our readers expect us to dispose the argument in a way that they can follow. If we have done our conceptual work well and have disposed the argument following the guidelines we learned, the readers should be able to follow the argument without too much trouble. The function then of the formal appeal and a good disposition is to take the readers through a rational process that the readers have not traveled on their own. It is as if we are guides and our readers want to see something we find beautiful, but they have never hiked this path before. With some help they can hike the path and see what we want to show them. Hopefully, they find the journey as worthwhile as we do, but the point is that they would not have taken it on their own. They need a guide, and as their guide we want the journey to be as easy and straightforward as we can make it.

In addition to leading our readers through the reasoning, a good disposition of the argument will have the additional effect of increasing the readers' confidence in us as writers (ethos). Our readers will believe that we are sensible and fair, that we share their interests, and that they can trust us as their guides. I don't know if you have ever had the experience of arriving in an unfamiliar city and hailing a taxi. You get in and hope that the driver knows where he's going and will get you there as fast and directly as he can. You are never sure, but you hope the driver is not running up the meter by taking a circuitous route. Still, you are a bit nervous. You don't want your readers to be nervous. You don't want your readers to feel like you are taking them on an aimless ride. By making and keeping your contract with your reader and by disposing the argument in a reasonable and clear manner, you assure your readers that you can be trusted and that your reader is in good hands. Thus, disposition enhances the persuasive force of an argument because it increases the ethical appeal that you as a writer have.

But that's not all disposing the argument well does. A good disposition of the argument also affects your readers (pathos). A well-disposed argument has a certain force or trajectory or momentum all its own. If the momentum of the argument is established by its disposition, at some point the reader ceases to worry about you the writer and starts to enjoy the argumentative force itself. The reader starts to go along for the ride and take pleasure in its movement. You may have had the experience of going on a ride at an amusement park. At first you are nervous, but after a while you stop worrying and start to enjoy the ride. A well-disposed argument can have this same effect on the reader. The reader gains confidence in the argument itself and enjoys the argumentative momentum. Thus, a well-disposed argument has an effect on the reader's attitude not just toward you, the writer, but also toward the argument itself. The reader begins to have confidence in the argument.

A well-disposed argument increases the reader's confidence in you the writer and in the argument itself to be sure, but that's not all. It has one other effect on the reader. If you can establish a momentum or trajectory in your argument, and if the reader begins to have confidence in the argument, at some point before you conclude the essay, the reader is likely to make a prediction as to where the argument is going. The reader will begin to sense the final destination and look for landmarks to verify his or her prediction.

You have most likely taken a long trip in a car. If you have never been along the route before, the journey seems to drag on and on. Eventually somebody will ask, "Are we there yet?" This is a question of boredom. You don't want your readers asking themselves, "Are we there yet?" If you have disposed the argument well and the readers can feel the momentum of the argument, they can sense where you are going and know where the destination is. In this case, the readers approach the final paragraphs of the argument with a sense of anticipation, wanting to verify that they know what's around the next turn. And when they arrive, they have the pleasure of knowing that they were right. But this is exactly how you want your readers to feel. You want them to feel that they are right at arriving at the destination that you wanted to lead them to. If you have disposed the argument well, the very disposition will allow your readers the pleasure of saying, "I told you so."

CONCLUSION

Disposition sometimes gets slighted when talking about writing. But in an argument what I hope you have seen is that the disposition is an essential part of the argument; it is part of the argument's persuasive force. By understanding the power of form and the guidelines of disposing an argument, you can meet your readers' expectations for form and reasonableness. If you meet your readers' expectations for form and reasonableness, you will keep your readers reading and will be able to lead them through the entire reasoning process as clearly and as straightforwardly as you can. In addition, you increase the readers' confidence in you as a reasonable, trustworthy person. You increase the reader's confidence in the argument, and you allow the reader the pleasure of beating you to your own conclusion. What could be better than that!

REFERENCE

Burke, K. (1968). *Counter-statement.* Berkeley, CA: University of California Press.

NOTES

NOTES

9
STYLE AND
DELIVERY

Letting the Light Shine
Through

Deborah Harrison

INTRODUCTION

I remember sitting in my first college English class waiting to get back my first college essay. I had sweated over that essay, spending hours thinking about it and writing it. When I got my essay back I quickly riffled through the pages to look at the grade and the comments on the last page. "Wonderful ideas." That was good. She liked my ideas. "Rather pretentious language." Wait a minute. What did that mean? Hadn't I written exactly how my high school teachers had taught me to write for college? I'd been careful to be formal and I'd thrown in big words and everything. Wasn't that what teachers wanted? That first essay was my initial awakening to the whole idea of style and delivery—and how much they matter in presenting "wonderful ideas."

Can't a brilliant idea speak for itself? Yes and no. What we have to say *and* how we say it matter in persuading an audience. Whenever we write, we enter into a conversation with our readers. It is an odd conversation, to be sure, because both writer and reader are alone; we write in private and readers read in private. The readers can't hear our voice, see our passion for the topic, or ask us questions. As writers we can't force the readers to keep reading. But we can entice readers to continue reading with the freshness of our ideas and the ease of our presentation. We can keep readers from becoming lost or bored. Our task as writers is to think deeply and clearly and to present our ideas in such a way that our readers understand our point of view. That takes good ideas *and* style and delivery.

WHAT IS STYLE?

Style is an elusive term. It has something to do with the idea to be expressed and the individuality of the writer (Harmon & Holman, 2000, p. 500). It encompasses clarity and coherence and conciseness and voice. But it adds up to more than these individual considerations. The essayist E. B. White said, "Style results more from what a person is than from what he knows" (as cited in Murray, 2001, p. 77). And since no two personalities are the same, no two styles are exactly the same. Just as we have our own style of dressing or talking, we have our own style of writing. Our style is made up of the choices we make in presenting our ideas. Do we write longer sentences or shorter sentences, have a chatty style or a more formal approach, use larger words or slang terms? Most of these choices will depend upon the rhetorical situation, upon the subject we are writing about and the audience we are writing to. But even if we change from more formal to informal writing, there is still something that is inherently ours that should shine through our writing.

CLARITY

The first requirement of any writing is that it communicate clearly. In fact, clarity trumps everything. If our readers don't understand what we are saying, then it's a given that they also won't be persuaded to our point of view. Being clear is the ability to express our thoughts in an understandable manner, the ability to reach out to our readers and put us both on the same page.

Clarity is never an easy task; we often don't know exactly what we want to say until after we've written it. Writing forces us to think. The process of writing *is* thinking. That's why clarity usually comes with rewriting. We plop down our ideas on the page, then we go back, once we've understood exactly what we mean to say, and make sure our ideas are clear for our readers.

The ancient rhetoricians had a telling definition of clarity. The Latin terms for clarity (*lucere* "to shine," *perspicere* "to see through,") suggest that clarity once meant language that allowed meaning to "'shine through,' like light through a window" (Crowley & Hawhee, 2004, p. 281). I like that metaphor, the idea of meaning shining through to our readers unimpeded. However, that kind of clarity usually comes at a price—hard work. George M. Trevelyan (1913), a distinguished British historian, backs me up on this point:

> The idea that histories which are delightful to read must be the work of superficial temperaments, and that a crabbed style betokens a deep thinker or conscientious worker, is the reverse of the truth. What is easy to read has been difficult to write. The labor of writing and rewriting, correcting and recorrecting, is the due exacted by every good book from its author. . . . The easily flowing connections of sentence with sentence and paragraph with paragraph has always been won by the sweat of the brow. (p. 34)

Deep or complex ideas need not be expressed in obscure ways. Indeed, they *shouldn't* be.

COHERENCE

"If there is any way for your readers to get lost—they will" (Hairston & Keene, 2003, p. 72). It is true. And it is a good thing to keep in mind because if readers do get lost, it is usually the writer's fault. The burden of communicating falls decisively at the feet of the writer. That is why the ability to connect ideas in a logical manner is so important in the process of persuasion.

A coherent essay is one that simply makes sense; it moves logically and smoothly from idea to idea. In the ideal essay, our "wonderful ideas" fit together like links on a chain. Each link is attached to the link before it and the link after it. There are no holes, no gaps. The readers move smoothly and easily from one point to the next. It is this connection of ideas in our essays that establishes the logic behind our arguments.

One way writers achieve coherence is through the expected three-part structure of an essay (see the discussion of **form** in the previous chapter). Readers expect an introduction, body, and conclusion. Most students, assuming they know this structure, arrive at college fully equipped with the five-paragraph essay. They can pull it out and slap it down in an evening: they write an introduction with a thesis, a body of three paragraphs that supports the thesis, and a conclusion that restates the thesis. However, what most students don't realize is that they are not tied to a five-paragraph essay. There are other ways to work with and look at an essay's structure. The five-paragraph essay is a good beginning. But it is not the end. It is a foundation upon which to build.

Keith Hjortshoj (2001) presents another approach to the three-part structure of an essay in his book *The Transition to College Writing*. He compares an essay to a journey we take with our readers. We start at the departure point—making sure our readers know where we are beginning the journey, and why. The body of the essay is the journey itself, carrying the readers smoothly from the point of departure through connected passages (usually more than three paragraphs) until we arrive at a destination. The destination takes us somewhere a little different than where we started—a culminating illumination or insight the readers can now thoroughly embrace because of the journey that led us there (pp. 32–46).

It should be quite clear how the path from the point of departure gets us to the destination. One of the ways writers keep us on the path is by moving smoothly from idea to idea with transition words like *for example, however, first, next,* and *finally.* These words help to guide the reader through the journey. They are the glue that holds ideas together. Notice the difference that exists in the following paragraph from a student essay when the transitions are removed. The first paragraph lacks transitions while the second paragraph retains them.

> Jazz bands began to split into two main categories: black and white. Black bands (bands made up entirely of African-Americans) were known as "big bands." Solos were

encouraged among all of the band members, not just the leader of the band. These bands played mostly for the poorer, lower class blacks of the era. These big bands began writing their own music. The music performed by jazz bands had been made up entirely of arrangements of the day's popular music. Music was written specifically for a band.

Now read the second paragraph with the transitions and note the difference in coherence and flow.

Jazz bands began to split into two main categories: black and white. Black bands (bands made up entirely of African-Americans) were known as "big bands" and *were characterized by a number of things. First,* solos were encouraged among all of the band members, not just the leader of the band. *Second,* these bands played mostly for the poorer, lower class blacks of the era. And *third,* these big bands began writing their own music. *Up until this time,* the music performed by jazz bands had been made up entirely of arrangements of the day's popular music. *It wasn't until this time* that music was written specifically for a band. [Emphasis added.]

The first paragraph seems disjointed. We don't understand how one idea connects to the next. But when transition words are supplied, the ideas link together smoothly, helping readers follow the logic of the ideas.

A colleague of mine compares transition words to markers on a trail. When we hike, we usually watch for markers along the trail to assure us we are on the right path and to encourage us in our journey. The markers let us know how far we have come and how much farther we have to go. They are visual reminders of our progress, and we come to depend on them for a sense of where we are on the path. Transition words in essays are like these markers on a trail: they clearly signal to the reader where we are on the path.

Another way writers keep us on the path is by repeating words that reinforce the relationship of one idea to another. This is accomplished by repeating information that is known before adding new information, thereby creating coherence as well as **cohesion** (see the previous chapter). Notice the links a student writer forges through this type of repetition in the following paragraph:

> The story of how jazz came about begins in New Orleans, Louisiana, around *the turn of the century. During this time,* numerous small bands were commissioned to play for funeral processions as they walked to the *tombs. On the way to the tombs,* the bands would play somber, mournful, music. However, *on the way back,* they would perform more *upbeat* tunes, celebrating the deceased person's life. It was this *upbeat* funeral music that became what we know today as jazz.

It is difficult to get lost when each idea links so clearly to the next. The first words of the second sentence, "During this time," refer to the last words of the first sentence, "the turn of the century." By building on information already presented, we as writers can move the readers along smoothly to a new idea, that "small bands were commissioned to play for funeral processions as they walked to the tombs." Many teachers refer to this as the "flow" of an essay. This flow is what allows us as writers to present the logic of our ideas to our readers in a seamlessly clear manner.

Another important way writers create coherence is by being specific. If we make a general statement, we'd better illustrate it with a specific example (or examples) so we are absolutely positive our readers understand our point. For instance, if we say reading helps to develop imagination, we should back that statement up with scientific research, or personal experience, or examples of when (and how) reading has done this for people. We might cite how the Harry Potter books awakened imagination in children, or we could quote a study with statistics to prove our point. Sweeping generalizations may sound grand, but they do little to clarify and still less to persuade. The more specific we are, the more we can be assured our intended meaning will be understood.

Structure, transitions, repetition, and specifics all help to create coherence that allows us to present our arguments clearly to our readers. Without coherence, our readers get lost and rarely arrive at the same destination as the writer. As William Zinsser (1976) puts it, "If the reader is lost, it is generally because the writer has not been careful enough to keep him on the path" (p. 8). Keeping readers on the right path with clarity and coherence is essential in writing an effective argument.

CONCISENESS

When we write, we want the most amount of power from the least amount of words. This is not to say, however, that we should get rid of words willy-nilly—just unnecessary ones. Some words are part of our style, create coherence, or are needed for the beauty and rhythm of language. But other words simply cloud our intended meaning, causing our readers to fumble about in a fog while they try to figure out what we are trying to say.

Let's look at a possible opening sentence for an essay on *Walden:*

> Henry David Thoreau argues in *Walden* that men spend their lives in "quiet desperation" due to the fact that they are overly preoccupied and busy with lots of things that are of little real value.

When we get rid of all the unnecessary words the sentence has more power because it allows the idea to shine through more clearly.

> Henry David Thoreau argues in *Walden* that men spend their lives in "quiet desperation" because they are preoccupied with things of little value.

We shouldn't use a sentence when a phrase will do; we shouldn't use three words when one word will do. *Due to the fact that* can be replaced with *because; preoccupied* and *busy* mean roughly the same thing, so we lose no meaning when we delete the redundancy. We should get rid of deadwood, those useless, floating pieces of language that clog up our sentences and add no meaning: *really, very, rather, so, quite.*

Conciseness in language eliminates the fog and gives our ideas more power. As the stylist William Strunk says, "Vigorous writing is concise. A sentence should contain no unnecessary words, a paragraph no unnecessary sentences, for the same reason that a drawing should have no unnecessary lines and a machine no unnecessary parts" (1979, p. 23).

VOICE

Voice is probably the first thing I look for in deciding whether I will continue to read something or not. What do I mean by voice? I mean that you, your personality, or how you want readers to perceive you comes off the page, that I can hear you speaking in your own matchless way, that I can feel you genuinely wish to engage me as your reader. It means there is a quality and genuineness to the writing that sets you apart from all other writers. Voice is like putting your thumbprint on anything you write. If you were to enter my house and steal my television, but you left your thumbprint on my wall, I could track you down and find you (and recover my television) because no one in the world has your exact thumbprint. We should have our thumbprint on everything we write. We shouldn't put aside who we are when we pick up a pen to write. Even if we are writing formal essays we can still maintain our voice, though it will be more subdued.

The first essay I wrote for my first college class lacked voice. That's what my professor meant when she said, "Rather pretentious language." My high school teachers had taught me to write so formally in preparation for college that I had all but obliterated my own voice. It took me many years to find it again. When I teach the concept of voice to my students, I encourage them to discover their own voices if they have lost them (or never found them). I assure them that their voice matters, and it can make a difference in the world. This concept seems to lift a burden from their shoulders. It is as if I have released them from a self-imposed prison: "I matter. My voice matters." Indeed it does.

Writing that has voice is far more engaging than writing that lacks it. Consider the following response on the topic "Education":

Education is of paramount importance in today's society. Young people today simply can't make it without a college education. A college education teaches young adults how to think, manage time, and be well rounded individuals. College students shouldn't take their education for granted but should work hard so they can succeed in today's world.

This response could have been written by any number of people. It does not have the voice of an individual shining through it, and therefore it fails to engage us as readers. Donald Murray (2001) has identified several other reasons that cause writing to lack voice: no intellectual challenge, no emotional challenge, no flow of energy that propels the readers forward (pp. 69–70). The response on education suffers from all of these maladies. Besides not having an individual personality coming through the writing, the paragraph lacks intellectual depth and emotional appeal. The author has said nothing new or interesting about education and so fails to engage the reader, one of the functions of voice. The writing makes sense, it flows, but it is boring—thus it doesn't propel us forward with anticipation for the next idea.

If voice makes such a difference in writing, how might we go about finding our voice? By being willing to be ourselves, by being willing to be honest, vulnerable, passionate. Notice the delightful yet quite diverse voices that emerge in the following samples.

> The primary difference between men and women is that women can see extremely small quantities of dirt. Not when they're babies, of course. Babies of both sexes have a very low awareness of dirt, other than to think it tastes better than food. (Barry, 1988, p. 219)

> On a morning in May 1804, there arrived at the White House . . . a visitor from abroad: an aristocratic young German, age thirty-four, a bachelor, occupation scientist and explorer. And like Halley's comet or the white whale or other such natural phenomena dear to the nineteenth century, he would be remembered by all who saw him for the rest of their days. (McCullough, 1992, p. 3)

My husband and I got married at eight in the morning. It was winter, freezing, the trees encased in ice and a few lone blackbirds balancing on telephone wires. We were in our early 30s, considered ourselves hip and cynical, the types who decried the institution of marriage even as we sought its status. (Slater, 2006, p. 32)

All of these samples are well written and effective. Barry's voice is informal and humorous. McCollough's voice is more formal, with longer sentences and bigger words, yet there is a pleasure in the refined tone. Slater's voice is engaging—promising well thought out insights and stark honesty. Who these authors are shines through their writing and sets their writing apart as their own. It is unlikely that anyone would mistake Barry's writing for McCullough's. It should be just as unlikely that anyone would mistake our writing for another's.

Our voice begins to come off the page with the first words we write. The title is usually a good indication of what we can expect from an essay. A good title should tantalize us to want to read more. Walker Percy puts it well: "A good title should be like a metaphor: It should intrigue without being too baffling or too obvious" (as cited in Trimble, 2000, p. 180). For example, a humanities class was assigned to write an essay arguing whether the cathedrals in the Middle Ages should have been humbly built and adorned or richly built and adorned (as they were). One student entitled her essay, "Forget the Poor—I Want a Gold Door." Another entitled it "Cathedrals in the Middle Ages." Which essay would you want to read first? As Geoffrey Parsons so clearly explains, "I place great emphasis on a title and a first sentence. You must think of your potential reader as a shy and reclusive trout. . . . Your task, is to cast a fly so vivid and appealing that forgetting all else he will leap at your bait" (as cited in Trimble, 2000, p. 180). Voice helps this leap to occur.

Another consideration in creating voice is what person to write in. Which person we choose, either first, second, or third person, affects the distance we create between ourselves and our readers. Depending on what our relationship is to our subject or our audience, we might want to lessen or widen the distance from our readers. For instance, the choice to write in first person (I, we) creates less distance between the writer and reader. It is less formal and more conversational. Using *we* distinctly lessens the distance because now the readers are included and feel a part of what is being said. However, while the first person lessens distance, it can sometimes lessen authority since it is less formal. Second person speaking (you) can be a tricky choice. If done well, the use of *you* can be seen as informal and chatty—and bring the audience closer. Done poorly, it can take on an authoritative, even superior, tone that can create distance since it can come across like a lecture—and few people enjoy being lectured. The third person choice (he, she, they, one) pushes the subject to the forefront, since references to the writer or reader disappear. This choice is more formal and creates the most distance between the writer and reader, but it can also establish more authority as the facts are allowed to speak for themselves.

Notice the change in tone and distance that occurs when the following narrative is changed from the first person to the third person.

> As I remember it, my story always starts out like a fairy tale. . . . Once upon a time in Paris, between two world wars, there lived a happy little boy. I was that little boy. (Lusseyran, 1987, p. 5)

> As he remembers it, his story always starts out like a fairy tale. . . . Once upon a time in Paris, between two world wars, there lived a happy little boy. He was that little boy.

In this case, there is far more power in the first example than in the second. The first example engages us in a real story; the second distances us from it as we stand back to observe it.

Choice of tense also affects voice and distance. The present tense has more immediacy than the past tense, since it gives readers a sense of participating in events as they are unfolding. The past tense can make readers feel that they are only standing back and observing events that have already happened. Notice the difference that tense makes in the following two sentences:

The boy reaches into his pocket and takes out a coin.

The boy reached into his pocket and took out a coin.

In the first sentence we feel that we are there, watching the boy pull out the coin. In the second sentence, we feel as if it has already happened and we are just standing back observing what has occurred.

Word choice and levels of formality can also affect the sense of voice. It is fine to use a big word if the big word is the right word. However, throwing around big words just to sound smart doesn't usually improve a writer's credibility. The use of the word *paramount* in the paragraph on "Education" sounds educated but lacks power since we're not even sure the writer knows what *paramount* means. But using a big word that is the right word is also the right choice. Mark Twain is quoted as saying, "The difference between the right word and the almost right word is like the difference between lightning and the lightning bug" (as cited in Marlowe, 2001). We want the right word to carry our intended meaning to our audience. If we change our words, we also change how our audience interprets our meaning. For instance, if we want to say that something needs to be done, it matters whether we choose to use the word *imperative, necessary* or *helpful* to convey that message. The different word choices convey a different sense of urgency.

We also need to pay attention to the level of formality in our writing. How much formality do we need to reel in our audience and have them accept our points? There is danger in writing too formally (we bore or lose our readers) or too informally (we could offend or lose credibility). Usually choosing the middle ground, what Wilma and David Ebbitt call the General English style, is the best choice, leaning a little to one side or the other as the topic or audience demands (1990, xiv–xv). In the General English style we avoid the dangers of falling into clichés (dark as night), slang terms (cool, hot), colloquialisms (Oh, my gosh), or sounding so formal that we could be stuffed and hung up to dry (It behooves me to remind you that your rent is inordinately past due).

Writing that has voice is more engaging and enhances meaning. The early Greek rhetoricians must have understood this concept, since originally in Greek the word *logos* meant "voice" or "speech." It was only later that logos also came to be associated with reason (Crowley & Hawhee, 2004, p. 20). Thus, voice and reason work hand in hand. Voice adds magic to our ideas: "The magic of writing is that the voice arises from the spaces between the words as much as from the words themselves, carrying meaning to the reader" (Murray, 2001, p. 70). This magic helps to establish our credibility with our readers and can affect the emotional attachment that our readers have to our ideas. These issues are crucial in persuading an audience.

DELIVERY, DELIVERY, DELIVERY

There was an ancient orator who, when asked what was the most important part of effective rhetoric, said, "Delivery, delivery, delivery" (as cited in Lunsford, Ruszkiewicz & Walters, 2001, p. 292). Of course, he was referring to oral presentation, to body language and voice inflection. But the same could be said today about written communication. It's important to pay attention to the details of delivery, our punctuation, usage, and layout, so that our ideas can be more easily understood and accepted.

Consider for a moment the following letter that was a mass mailing to potential clients. The real estate agent is hoping to drum up business by persuading his audience that he is qualified to handle their real estate needs.

Dear Homeowner,

I would like to introduce myself. My name is_____. And I am a new real estate agent in the _____area. The past seven years I have been working as a Golf Professional. As a golf professional and working with a diverse group of clientele. I gained an invaluable experience in customer relations.

This is an exciting step for me and I would be thrilled to have you apart of it! If you have been thinking about buying or selling-residential or commercial; or if you know of anyone who is thinking of buying or selling a home. Give me a call, and let me help you with all of your real estate necessities.

It is possible that this individual *is* quite qualified to handle the real estate needs of his clientele—but his credibility is definitely compromised when he doesn't pay closer attention to the delivery of his letter. There are minor errors (capitalizing Golf Professional and including two periods) and there are major errors in sentence structure and punctuation. For instance, there are sentence fragments that impede understanding and cause the reader to have to reread for meaning: "As a golf professional and working with a diverse group of clientele." Where does this idea belong? With the sentence before it or the sentence after? And glaring punctuation errors also impede understanding: "If you have been thinking about buying or selling-residential or commercial; or if you know of anyone who is thinking of buying or selling a home" (the semicolon should actually be another dash—but it's a sentence fragment nonetheless). Even though the agent is obviously excited about his new career and is direct in his approach, because he hasn't taken the time to carefully craft and proofread the letter, many potential clients may arrive at the same conclusion: "If he doesn't take the time to attend to the details of a simple letter, how can I be sure I can trust him to attend to the details of my real estate transactions?" In other words, his lack of attention to delivery hurts his credibility and lessens his ability to persuade his audience. Just this morning a friend of mine called and mentioned that she had considered joining a particular online dating service but had decided against it when she noticed several obvious errors in spelling and punctuation. Does delivery matter in convincing an audience? It most definitely does.

Punctuation

Punctuation choices can affect our ability to persuade the reader. As with the letter from the real estate agent, our attention to the details of our written communication can affect both the logic of our ideas and the credibility of our ideas.

In matters of punctuation we have some advantages over our ancient counterparts in Greece and Rome. They had no punctuation marks. And what is even harder to imagine, all written works were done in *scriptio continua*, meaning that there weren't even spaces between the words. In classical times all writing was meant to be read out loud, whether in private or public, so learning how to read the words, where to put the appropriate pauses and emphasis, was an art that took practice. The first punctuation marks were created to help actors in Greek dramas know where to breathe. Later they were used by teachers to help their students learn how to read a text out loud. So the first punctuation marks were rhetorical and used to enhance oral interpretation.

When reading became a silent, private affair during the Middle Ages, punctuation marks were needed to guide the reader along. Charlemagne recognized that something needed to be done about the mess writing was in, so in A.D. 781 he asked his minister of education, Alcuin of York, to set things right. Alcuin set up a school that the monks attended, and by the ninth century we had a standardized writing style that included lower case letters, arrangement into sentences and paragraphs, and some punctuation marks (completetranslation.com, 2005). However, it wasn't until the invention of the printing press in 1436 that we finally started to solidify the marks of punctuation to help in silent reading. For nearly two hundred years printers tinkered with punctuation marks until by the 1700s the system we know today was generally in place.

Today, since most reading is done silently and alone, punctuation has become the subtle means by which we as authors can extend meaning to our readers. Since readers don't have the luxury of our facial gestures or tone, our punctuation must take up that slack. It is for this reason that I see punctuation as an art—not just as a collection of rules. Granted, there are rules that we must follow, but I like to think of punctuation as rules that help us know how to create tone and enhance meaning. Even the rules give us choices. In this light, punctuation becomes as much of an art form as painting or drawing. In these art forms, the choice to use a single line here or there can make considerable difference in how an art work is viewed or the feeling surrounding the work. For instance, a diagonal line in a drawing creates tension as the viewer waits for the line to right itself or fall. So it is with punctuation: a single choice of which punctuation mark to use in a given place can change the tone of the sentence or the actual meaning of the sentence. Take the following sentence, a popular example that has been used by teachers for years to demonstrate the value of punctuation:

A woman, without her man, is nothing.

A woman: without her, man is nothing.

In the first sentence a woman can't be without her man, but in the second, the man can't be without the woman. Quite a difference in meaning to convey with only punctuation marks! And consider the difference punctuation choice makes in the following example:

I must see him at once—at once, not later.

I must see him at once . . . at once, not later.

In the first sentence the dash gives boldness to the sentence; we can almost hear the speaker pounding on the desk. In the second sentence the ellipsis creates mystery, a pause for consideration.

Sometimes a punctuation mark may convey a special kind of meaning that cannot be achieved efficiently any other way. Lynne Truss (2003) gives an excellent example of the difference in meaning that punctuation choices can make in her book *Eats, Shoots, & Leaves.*

See how the sense changes with the punctuation in this example:

> Tom locked himself in the shed. England lost to Argentina.

These two statements as they stand, could be quite unrelated. They merely tell you two things have happened, in the past tense.

> Tom locked himself in the shed; England lost to Argentina.

We can infer from the semicolon that these events occurred at the same time, although it is possible that Tom locked himself in the shed because he couldn't bear to watch the match and therefore still doesn't know the outcome...

> Tom locked himself in the shed: England lost to Argentina.

All is now clear. Tom locked himself in the shed *because* England lost to Argentina. And who can blame him, that's what I say. (pp. 129–130)

The sentences remained the same. All that changed was the punctuation. But the punctuation changed the meaning and the tone. Only a semicolon can tell a reader that these two sentences are closely related in the writer's mind. Only a colon can inform the reader that what follows is a direct result of what came before. These are subtle nuances that punctuation can effectively convey.

It's important for us to know the rules—the accepted conventions—but it's also important for us to know when it is appropriate to bend those rules for our rhetorical purposes. The stylist Joseph Williams (2000) refers to this as learning to observe rules thoughtfully (pp. 20–21). I had experience with this whole idea of learning to observe rules thoughtfully when I was a teenager growing up in southern California. I had asked my dad, an avid tennis player, to teach me how to play tennis. The first thing he did was put the tennis racket in my hand and say, "This racket is an extension of your arm. You no longer have a wrist. If a ball comes at you low, don't break your wrist to hit it back, but bend down from your knees to meet it so that you can hit it back without bending your wrist." I believed him. I learned my backhand and forehand and was coming along nicely—until we were practicing one hot Saturday afternoon.

The heat was taking its toll and sweat was trickling down the side of my face. I began to get tired of bending down to meet all those low balls. Then I noticed that my dad wasn't doing what he had told me to do. When I hit a ball low over the net, he bent his wrist and just whisked it back at me—without bending down to meet it. *Well*, I thought to myself, *I'm hot, I'm tired, I'm going to bend my wrist, too.* So I did. For the next ball that came to me. But it didn't go over the net. It just bounced back miserably and landed at my feet. Not to be discouraged, I tried it again when a ball came over low—with the same results. My dad glared at me over the net. He hit the next ball very hard and very low, and when I failed to return that ball as well (admittedly, I was a slow learner), he motioned to me to meet him at the net and he came striding forward to deliver his lecture. It was a simple one. "You can't break the rules until you know the rules. Now go back and hit the ball the way I taught you!" He had been playing tennis for forty years by that time and he understood perfectly what it took to get the ball back over the net. I, on the other hand, was a beginner, and I didn't yet know enough to break the rules and still have them work for me.

The same is true of the conventions of English—particularly punctuation rules. We need to know the rules so well that we understand when it is appropriate, for our purposes, to break those rules. For instance, many teachers preach about the sins of sentence fragments and tell their students to avoid fragments at all costs. However, a sentence fragment can actually carry great power—if it is used appropriately. The real estate agent used a sentence fragment that didn't carry power: "As a golf professional working with a diverse group of clientele." This is because the fragment caused confusion, most likely because the author didn't realize he was using a fragment. I used a fragment in telling the tennis story: "So I did. *For the next ball that came to me.*" I did it on purpose. I did it because I felt the fragment would create more emphasis and thus more power. The truth is that most great writers use fragments for effect. The difference is that these writers know they are using a fragment and they know what effect they want to create with that fragment. They also know when the formality of the subject matter or the audience would render a fragment inappropriate. They have learned to "observe rules thoughtfully."

It matters that we understand the rules of punctuation and that we use them with judgment and good taste. Using punctuation well helps to establish credibility with our readers. Sometimes it is quite clear what punctuation marks should be used—an obvious rule that dictates what is right or wrong. At other times we may have many choices that are acceptable, each with their accompanying tone and subtle nuance of meaning. In these instances, we'll need to rely on our common sense for the best choice. In the end, we simply want our readers to understand our intended message. Effective punctuation helps us achieve this goal.

USAGE AND LAYOUT

As with any written communication, it's important to always keep in mind the audience we are addressing and the purpose for which we are addressing them. In the back of our minds we should keep the constant nagging thought that ultimately we are writing to persuade someone of something. How best to do that? Style matters, as we have already discussed, as do punctuation choices. But we should keep in mind a few other considerations of delivery: usage and layout.

Usage has to do with how we actually use the language, our choice of appropriate words. Some people think of it as linguistic etiquette. Just as we probably wouldn't choose to show up in sweats and an old T-shirt for a formal dinner to meet our future in-laws, we shouldn't choose language that will offend or distance our audience from us. We should always write to be inclusive of gender, race, or ethnic groups.

Before the Feminist Movement of the '60s and '70s, the so-called generic "he" was used to refer to both male and female. Since that time, however, the generic "he" has fallen out of grace, and all careful writers avoid its use in favor of more inclusive terms. Probably the easiest way to include everyone is to use the plural—either "they" or "we." But if writers choose to use the singular, they must also be careful to include both "he and she" in all their writing. The following sentence, for example, does not use inclusive language:

A good writer knows that *he* should strive for clarity.

This sentence can easily be rewritten to include everyone without sacrificing style or meaning:

Good writers know that they should strive for clarity.

We know that writers should strive for clarity.

A good writer knows that he or she should strive for clarity.

Why does including everyone matter? Some readers might become offended or be so caught up in how we are saying things that they miss what we are trying to say—and therefore are never persuaded to our point of view. An example. I was reading through an article in a magazine that was encouraging me, as a parent, to help increase my child's vocabulary by entering my child in a vocabulary contest that offered scholarships to college.

A strong vocabulary helps kids score higher on SATs, gives them an advantage on college admissions and can even help them win thousands of dollars in college scholarships. So what are you waiting for? Sign your child up . . . and get *him* started. ("Give Your Child the Verbal Edge," 2005, p. 12) [Emphasis added.]

Wait, wait, wait. *Him?* Only boys? Are girls excluded? Not as bright? Is the article suggesting that my daughters aren't as intelligent or as capable as my sons? That girls aren't as good as boys? That as a female I'm inferior? As you can see, I've gotten so caught up in a word choice that I've missed the main point, which is that my children could improve their vocabulary and win scholarships. It is possible to become so caught up in word choices that the intended audience misses the point altogether. We want to avoid that by choosing our words carefully. We should always try to be inclusive in our language.

Similarly, we should be careful to avoid any unnecessary references to race or ethnic groups. If these points of information are not relevant to our argument then we should leave the information out of our remarks. If race or ethnic group is pivotal to our argument then we need to be careful to refer to the race or ethnic group in the manner they prefer (is *black* more appropriate in this instance or *African American?*) and we need to be sure our handling of the information is fair and doesn't fall into stereotypes. For instance, it would be unfair (and untrue) to suggest that all Arabs are terrorists. Our goal is to draw in our audience so they will be persuaded by our penetrating ideas and our obvious good sense; we do not wish to exclude or offend our audience, distancing them from us and our ideas.

Another consideration of delivery is to take care with the visual **layout** of a written argument. A good page layout is a type of persuasion in and of itself. It persuades us initially that we want to read the page. It shows that the writer cares enough about what he or she is writing to consider all aspects of the presentation of the idea. Is the page visually appealing and does the white space invite reading? If we use visuals, are they appropriately placed within the text? Are the paragraphs so long they are daunting? Is the font distracting? While we usually stay with Times Roman font for all academic papers, it is possible to use *italic* typeface for emphasis within the text. Italics calls attention to the words in a refined manner (Do it *now*). In an academic paper, using all capitals for emphasis (DO IT NOW) is overkill, as is bolded (Do it **now**) and overuse of exclamation points (Do it now!!!). In addition, if a paper is longer it is often helpful for readers to have headings and subheadings to "chunk" information together for easier digestion, as has been done in this chapter with the major heading "What is Style?" and the subheadings "Clarity," "Coherence," "Conciseness," and "Voice." Headings can make it easier to identify the main points and to more clearly understand how they fit together.

CONCLUSION

When I wrote my first college essay, so many years ago, I had not understood the value of style and delivery in presenting my "wonderful ideas." I had not understood how much style and delivery matter in creating credibility, meaning, and emotion. I understand their value now, and work hard to present ideas clearly and coherently to my readers. As writers we should try to make the journey for our readers a pleasurable one, where they don't get lost in the fog, or bored, or distanced from our ideas. We should strive for the clarity the Greeks alluded to, one that allows meaning to shine through unimpeded to the readers.

REFERENCES

Barry, D. (1988). Batting clean-up and striking out. In *Dave Barry's greatest hits,* (p. 219). New York: Crown.

Complete translation. (n.d.). *A history of punctuation.* Retrieved March 18, 2005, from http://www.completetranslation.com/punctuation.htm

Crowley, S. & Hawhee, D. (2004). *Ancient rhetorics for contemporary students* (3rd ed.). New York: Pearson Longman.

Ebbitt, W. R. & Ebbitt, D. (1990). *Index to English* (8th ed.) New York: Oxford University Press.

Give your child the verbal edge—and a scholarship. (2005, September). *Reader's Digest,* 12.

Hairston, M. & Keene, M. (2003). *Successful writing* (5th ed.). New York: W. W. Norton.

Harmon, W. &. Holman, C. H. (2000). *A handbook to literature.* (8th ed.). Upper Saddle River, NJ: Prentice Hall.

Hjortshoj, K. (2001). Footstools and furniture. In *The transition to college writing.* (pp. 32–46). Boston, MA: Bedford/St. Martin's.

Lusseyran, J. (1987). *And there was light.* New York: Parabola.

Lunsford, A. & Ruszkiewicz, J. (2001). *Everything's an argument.* Boston: Bedford/St. Martin's.

Marlowe, M. E. (Ed.). (2001). *The importance of words.* Retrieved March 24, 2006, from http:www.bible-researcher.com/language-quotes.html

McCullough, D. (1992). Journey to the top of the world. In *Brave companions.* (pp. 3–19). New York: Touchstone.

Murray, D. M. (2001). *The craft of revision* (4th ed.). Boston, MA: Thomson Heinle.

Slater, L. (2006, February) True love. *National Geographic,* 32–49.

Strunk, W. M. (with White, E. B.). (1979). *Elements of style* (3rd ed.) New York: Macmillan Publishing.

Trevelyan, G. M. (1913). *Clio, a muse and other essays literary and pedestrian.* London: Longman.

Trimble, J. R. (2000). *Writing with style* (2nd ed.). Upper Saddle River, NJ: Prentice-Hall.

Truss, L. (2003). *Eats, shoots, & leaves.* New York: Gotham Books.

Williams, J. M. (2000). *Style.* (6th ed.). New York: Longman.

Zinsser, W. (1976). *On writing well.* New York: Harper & Row.

NOTES